Praise for Jen Sincero

"In the world of life coaching, Jen Sincero is the Royal Badass." —Associated Press

"Sincero brings a fun, feminine verve to now well-tread self-help tropes. . . . The tone is far more feisty than academic, and there's humor on every page, all of which is exactly what her intended audience most needs." —*Publishers Weekly*

"*You Are a Badass* will silence your inner critic and help you build a life worthy of the kind of Facebook news feed that others envy. Take a day off from looking for your inner goddess and spend some time cultivating your outer badass instead." —*Bustle*

"If I could only recommend one book to you, [*You Are a Badass*] would be it. This book will make you feel ready to take on the world, and smash your baggage in the process. It's like having a personal pep talk in your hands." —*Forbes*

"Sincero writes in a conversational, witty tone that actually makes self-improvement sound fun." —*PureWow*

"As soon as we picked up the *New York Times* bestseller [*You Are a Badass*], Sincero's honest, funny, and down-to-earth take on tackling life's challenges kept us turning pages." —*StyleCaster*

BADASS
HABITS

CULTIVATE THE CONFIDENCE,
BOUNDARIES, AND KNOW-HOW
TO UPGRADE YOUR LIFE

JEN SINCERO

life

PENGUIN BOOKS
An imprint of Penguin Random House LLC
penguinrandomhouse.com

First published in the United States of America by Viking,
an imprint of Penguin Random House LLC, 2020
Published in Penguin Books 2021

A Penguin Life Book

Library of Congress Control Number: 2020943738

ISBN 9781984877437 (hardcover)
ISBN 9781984877451 (paperback)
ISBN 9781984877444 (ebook)

Printed in the United States of America
5   7   9   10   8   6

Set in Bembo MT Pro
Designed by Cassandra Garruzzo

PENGUIN LIFE

BADASS HABITS

Jen Sincero is a world-renowned author, success coach, and motivational speaker who has spent more than a decade helping people transform their lives and their bank accounts.

ALSO BY JEN SINCERO

*You Are a Badass Every Day: How to Keep Your Motivation Strong,
Your Vibe High, and Your Quest for Transformation Unstoppable*

You Are a Badass at Making Money: Master the Mindset of Wealth

*You Are a Badass: How to Stop Doubting
Your Greatness and Start Living an Awesome Life*

The Straight Girl's Guide to Sleeping with Chicks

Don't Sleep with Your Drummer

To Mother Earth

CONTENTS

BADASS
HABITS

INTRODUCTION

When I first decided to write a book about habits, the topic seemed like such a natural follow-up to the other Badass books. In the original *You Are a Badass*, I mentioned this little truism: *Our thoughts become our words, our words become our beliefs, our beliefs become our habits, and our habits become our realities.* Habits are the only piece of the equation I had yet to delve into deeply, and I couldn't wait to get crackin'. That is, until the following conversation with myself crawled up and sat on my chest:

> *Me:* Habits! Of course! Why, they're the very sculptors of our realities! I'm going to write the fuck out of this book.

> *Me, enjoying a tower of onion rings, a few days after giving up fried food:* Are we going to write about how to purchase a gym membership and never use it? Or how to not stop cursing? Because we could write the fuck out of that.
>
> *Me:* Oh my God, that's so true. My habits suck. What the hell am I thinking? I have the self-discipline of a toddler.

I began listing all of the reasons why I was unqualified, unable, and unauthorized to write this book; how I was about to tank my brand, insult my readers, and inspire my publisher to ask for its money back. Then I realized, *Oh look, I'm excelling at a habit right now, that most unsavory of human habits: focusing on the negative. I'm blowing past the fact that I haven't touched a cigarette in over two decades even though I love smoking more than I love most people; that I'm a highly accomplished flosser, hydrater, gratituder, writer, bed maker, meditator, and show-up-on-timer; and that I'll take a backpack and a high alpine trail over a stinky gym any day.* Cursing and fried food, however—there's still work to be done around cursing and fried food.

I bring this up because if you're reading this book with any skepticism about your stick-to-itiveness when it comes to habits, I want to remind you that nobody is perfect. And that we really can do anything we set our minds to (including things we've fake-set our minds to in the past). And that we all tend to sell ourselves short and focus on our failures instead of celebrating our victories. Even people who are successful beyond belief admit to occasionally letting negativity and feelings of inadequacy push them around. I've heard some say that every once in a while they'll forget how much they love what they do, ignore the standing ovations and rave reviews they receive from the outside world, and focus all their attention on that one stink-bomb hater on Instagram who thinks they suck, hand him the bullhorn, and let his opinion drown out the cheering crowds.

Mastering the powerful, positive mindset that's required to keep upping your habits game is all about staying aware, shifting your focus when you catch yourself wandering down Woe-Is-Me Lane, and consciously thinking thoughts that are aligned with where you want to go and who you want to become. When it comes to building great habits and ditching lousy ones, your commitment to staying focused on who you're becoming *regardless of where you are/who you are right now* is the mightiest power you've got.

> Contrary to popular belief, habits are more about who you're being than what you're doing.

One of the main reasons we don't stick to the habits we'd love to adopt, or permanently give the heave-ho to the habits we'd love to lose, is that we focus on taking action—which is important—but we don't get on board emotionally and mentally, which is more important. Then, when our new habits get challenging or boring (a favorite pastime of most habits thanks to the fact that they're so repetitive), we abandon them for something easier. Or something more fun. Or something that offers more immediate gratification. Or something that tastes really good with ketchup on it.

For example, let's say you've tried over and over to break your habit of spending more than you make. You've got a well-paying job and you put part of each paycheck toward your credit card bill and a little into your savings account and you carefully map out your budget each month. Then, in spite of your careful planning, you find yourself going on trips and forensically investigating furniture sales and jovially shouting "Drinks are on me!" and before you know it, your savings account is a ghost town and you're pleading on the phone with Pat at the collection agency again. Chances are excellent that deep down you're scared to stop overspending because you're trying to fill an emotional hole with stuff and experiences. Or maybe you come from a family full of spenders and you subconsciously worry you'll be judged and/or abandoned by them if you break with tradition and get your financial act together. It's essential when building good habits to focus on the whole enchilada—your head, your heart, and your hands—otherwise the meditating stops; the fingernails start being bitten again; your calm, sober repose at yet another passive-aggressive family gathering turns into "All right, I've had enough. Who wants to play Tequila Truth or Dare?!"

My hope is that this book offers some fresh perspectives on proven habit-forming processes and helps you dethrone whatever obstacles you've allowed to lord over you in the past. I also hope that it makes the whole habit-building-and-busting experience easier by boiling down a seemingly complex process and doling it out into manageable, bite-sized exercises that you implement one day at a time. I want you to get rolling and figure out which tools work best for you so you can start seeing real results—the kind of results you've yet to behold—that actually stick around. I'm a coach, not a scientist, so while ensmartening you is a goal, nothing gets me all teary-eyed and verklempt like the hallelujah of a dream realized. *You see? You see that black belt you just karated your way into? YOU did that. Here, hold my snacks. I've got to get a picture of this.*

I'll start by briefly explaining what habits are and how they work. I'll help you become aware of the habits you've already got (the good, the bad, and the ugly) and figure out which ones have got to go, which new ones you'd like to create, and who you need to start being in order to pull this all off. I'll also get you good at setting no-nonsense boundaries so you can alert your tribe, and yourself, that your needs are now a priority, that you're creating the space—emotionally and physically—to allow yourself to fully flourish, and that yes, this being good at setting boundaries thing is a habit you're going to keep (perhaps amid the indignant screams and protests of all those who are being booted out of first place).

Once we've got your heart and head on board, I'll help you pick one clearly defined habit to work on for the rest of the book. I'll walk you through a powerful 21-step process to either anchor in your new habit or permanently banish an old one, depending on what you choose. Ideally you'll take the process day by day over the course of three weeks in order to keep the beast of overwhelm at bay, give your new habit time to take hold, and keep the work as interesting as possible. The goal here is to have an interactive experience. I want you to hit the ground running and start becoming the person you're excited to become *while you're reading this book* instead of just becoming someone who now has a lot more information about what habits are. Or who understands the science behind how habits work. Or who knows how it feels to fall asleep with a book about habits lying on your face.

Please get a new notebook and dedicate it exclusively to the work we're about to do (no grocery lists), and start cultivating your new habit with a clean slate, focusing on the exciting new life that awaits you, as opposed to letting failures you've experienced in the past cloud your confidence. Who you desire to become is not only available to you but you're meant to become this upgraded version of yourself, otherwise you wouldn't have the desire in the first place and you sure as hell wouldn't be bothering with this book. Trust that each new day holds untold possibilities and remember:

> In every moment, you have the profound ability to make choices that will completely change your habits and your reality, either right away or over time.

Making powerful, life-altering choices is simply a habit, a habit that you've already started mastering.

GAVE UP BEING A LAZY ASS AND GOT IN SHAPE, JULIE, 60

My doctor told me I was headed for type 2 diabetes and that I needed to move more and try to lose some weight. I didn't like the sound of needing to be on meds my whole life and I also didn't like having a solid ten to fifteen pounds of extra blub in my club. So I decided that rain or shine, I could manage to exercise every morning before work on a yoga mat in my living room for at least fifteen minutes. How hard is that to do for my health?

I found a great online workout that was a combo of yoga, stretching, muscle strength, and cardio. Every morning I pulled that yoga mat out of the closet and I found that after stretching and doing some basic yoga moves, I was awake enough to do a little more. I did some strength-training exercises using my own body weight, and thought, *Geez, if I weighed less it wouldn't be so hard to hoist my petard off this mat!*

Three push-ups led to five to ten and now my daily routine is about thirty minutes total. As soon as I started doing this I began to feel better about myself.

I felt stronger. It kept me motivated and I now look forward to doing my workout at least five days a week.

At the same time, I started an online diet and health program that taught me about the psychology of why I eat and how to change my lifelong habits. This was an eye opener. "Mindless" eating versus "mindful" eating was huge. I learned to actually look at the food I was eating, not at the TV, to take a moment between bites and really taste what I was eating, not just chuck it down my gullet. I also learned to understand my personal hunger scale. When I wanted something to eat I would ask myself, *Am I actually hungry or just bored, stressed, sad, or agitated?* Another tip was not waiting until I was at Code Red–level starving on my hunger scale, because that means you grab anything from a vending machine or dive into the leftover donuts from the morning meeting. I learned other strategies and hacks. A big one was to always have healthy, yummy snacks in my bag, at work, and at home. If you're planning to eat dinner out, go online and look at the menu ahead of time and figure out what the best choice is and stick with it. Because otherwise, you'll see what everyone else is ordering and fly off the calorie rails.

The other big change of behavior for me was to start writing down everything I ate every day to be more mindful of what I was eating. And weighing myself every day. Sounds hideous, but it worked. It's now two years later and I've lost fifteen pounds (albeit slowly), but more importantly, I've kept it off. I continue to weigh myself every day and track my daily food. I have learned that this is what works for me. Of course there are days I go way over my calorie target for the day, but I don't get upset about it. I just adjust the next day. Believe me, I love food. And I still eat what I want. I just monitor my portion sizes and always try to tap into mindful eating, not mindless eating.

CHAPTER 1

WHO YOU'RE IN THE HABIT OF BEING

My brother Stephen and his wife, Jenny, came for a visit one year during Fiesta de Santa Fe, a historical celebration that attracts thousands of people to my New Mexican hometown every fall. We didn't participate in any of the festival's festivities during their stay, but we did brave the throngs of revelers in order to walk downtown and have ourselves some margaritas. The walk took us about forty-five minutes each way, and after a lovely afternoon of cocktailing we found ourselves back in my driveway just as the sun was setting. We stood around, taking in the reddening sky, slightly buzzed on tequila and the smug satisfaction of having made it all the way there and back on foot, when out of nowhere, Jenny started clutching at her throat as if she couldn't breathe. She'd suddenly realized, with horror, that somewhere along the way her diamond pendant had fallen off the chain around her neck and was lost.

My brother immediately flew into action. "I'll retrace our steps," he said, his eyes thoroughly scanning the ground beneath Jenny's feet before he slowly and methodically turned and headed back out my driveway. I began protesting that it would be dark in a matter of minutes, that he was high if he thought he could find her itty-bitty diamond among the sea of fallen leaves and hordes of people, but Jenny turned to me and said, "Let him go. He's weirdly amazing at finding shiny things. He's like a crow." So we stood and watched as Steve headed down my street and back into town, with nothing but his cell phone flashlight lighting his way and the thrill of the quest lighting his heart.

Meanwhile, Jenny and I got in my car and headed back to the bar to crawl around on the floor and see if we could find her pendant ourselves. On the way we passed Stephen, who simply raised his free hand in the air and waved when he heard us honk and holler, unwilling to take his eyes off the ground for even a second. After about ten minutes of trying, and failing, to find a parking place in the midst of the melee, I was about to give up and head back home when we got a text from my brother that read: "Found it!" To which I replied, "I don't believe you," to which he replied with a picture of himself standing in the middle of the street, each arm around a tourist he'd talked into posing with him, proudly holding Jenny's pendant in his front teeth. I later learned *it had been kicked off the sidewalk into someone's driveway and that he found it anyway.* My jaw hit the floor and has remained there ever since, but Jenny just shook her head and said, "I'm telling you, he's a crow. He finds shit all the time."

Steve used to have a job in the diamond business as a sorter. He'd spend his days in a room called "the pit" with a handful of other sorters, categorizing large piles of not-so-large diamonds according to the three *C*s—cut, carat, color—by holding each one up to a light with a pair of tweezers and looking at it through a loupe. While inspecting a diamond, it wasn't uncommon to accidentally tweeze it a bit too hard and send it ricocheting across the room—*doink!*—where it would land somewhere on the not-so-clean linoleum floor, on a shelf, or perhaps in someone's hair. There was no telling how many precious stones had gone missing in the pit over the years, and finding them became a perpetual Easter egg hunt, one that Steve participated in with vigor every time he put down his tweezers, for the two years that he worked there.

This is how, in the basement of a diamond wholesaler

on Forty-Seventh Street in New York City, Steve became the Patron Saint of Lost Shiny Things. His impressive résumé went on to boast of a diamond earring discovered on the floor of a crowded deli; a tennis bracelet spotted next to an ATM machine; countless coins, chains, keys, watches, precious stones; and one morning, while walking to the train, he found the necklace that Jenny (the Patron Saint of Broken Clasps) had lost three months before, nestled in the top of a snowbank.

Steve never zeroed in on the tiny, lost, and shiny until he worked in the diamond business. But thanks to that job, always being on the lookout—consciously and unconsciously—became a habit.

> Habits: no-brainers. A routine tendency or behavior. Knee-jerkery. Beliefs, thoughts, and actions that one repeats on autopilot.

Here are some of the key elements involved in habit creation:

1. **The Trigger.** Every time Steve took a pause from his work, it triggered his habit of scoping the room for lost

diamonds. Triggers send cues to our brains that it's time to perform a habit. A trigger can be a sound (the noise from an alarm clock triggers us to wake up and get out of bed), an action (finishing dinner is a trigger to light a ciggy), a thought *(It's four o'clock, so I reckon I should feed the dog)*, a feeling (when the temperature drops, you rub your arms to warm up), a smell (when you smell your neighbors BBQing, you casually swing by, *Oh, I didn't realize you were cooking, is this a bad time?*), a sight (seeing a person on the street is a trigger to say hello), or an emotion (feeling upset is a trigger to eat a cherry pie). Triggers begin a chain reaction that results in the completion of the habit. And the sequence goes a little sumthin' like this:

2. **The Sequence.** Our bodies are expert problem solvers, running around with a clipboard, making sure everything's working in the most efficient and productive manner possible: moving blood where it's needed most; breaking down food; healing broken bones and torn skin; sprouting hair and toenails; taking down disease; unleashing a flood of tears and obscenities when you accidentally drop your phone in the toilet. Habits are the body's way of lightening the load on our brains, of putting problem-solving on autopilot in order to free up room to take in more information and perform more

tasks. Habits work in a sequence of sorts that starts with the trigger (getting in the car), which signals a need (I don't want to die), which then leads to a habit or response (putting on a seat belt), which then leads to the reward (I feel snuggly and safe). Here are some more examples:

Trigger: Your dog walks into the room.

Need: To physically experience his insane cuteness.

Response/habit: Smothering, kissing, acting like a moron.

Reward: You feel happy.

Trigger: You're driving home from work.

Need: To live a longer, healthier life.

Response/habit: Stop at the gym and work out for forty-five minutes.

Reward: You feel invigorated and have a sense of accomplishment.

Trigger: Your divorce lawyer calls.

Need: To not throw a plate at the wall.

Response/habit: Pace around in circles and twirl your hair around your finger.

Reward: You feel calmer.

These are all examples of how triggers set your habits into motion, but triggers can also be used to help you quit bad habits, and I'll show you how to do that later in the book.

3. **Repetition.** Think of your brain as a jungle full of images and ideas and feelings all growing and twisting and tangling around one another as you gather more and more information throughout your life. Now imagine that all of your thought patterns and knee-jerk reactions and beliefs about the way things are have cut well-worn paths through this jungle in your mind, paths that you walk down every day, doop de do, without even needing to look where you're going. When you decide to make a change—*Hey, I'm no longer gonna be a lazy, out-of-shape person who secretly litters, I'm gonna step it up and get me some different habits*—repetition is the tool you'll use to hack through the vines, wrestle fallen trees out of your way, and forge a new path through the jungle of your mind.

Repetition of your new habit will require some mental and physical effort at first, but the scales on the piano that you struggle to remember and execute become second nature after you've played them three hundred times; tying your shoes after decades of doing it takes zero thought these days; answering questions with a

You betcha, tiger! unconsciously comes flying out of your mouth after making fun of Grandma for saying it your whole life. I'm so in the habit of calling my mother to check in on her when I get in my car each morning that I once dialed her up while she was sitting right next to me, in town for a visit.

> When you repeat something enough times, you establish new neural pathways in the brain that your habit flows through effortlessly and automatically, allowing you to literally fuggetaboutit.

Take a moment right now to think about something you used to struggle with that's now a habit—working your cell phone, shaving, hitting a tennis ball, driving a car, respecting your neighbor Sarah's wishes that you refer to her as Desert Flower from now on. It's nearly impossible to remember all the little details you used to have to keep in mind when you were anchoring in this-behavior-that's-now-a-habit, because you literally changed the wiring of your brain through repetition.

4. **Ease.** It's no big surprise to discover that the easier things are, the more likely we are to do them. This goes for the habits we'd like to form, the habits we'd like to break, and the habits we don't even realize we've signed up for (which, believe you me, account for an alarming amount of them—thanks, Mom and Dad!). My brother didn't set out to be the guy who finds sparkly stuff that most people don't see; he developed the habit because it was easy, it was fun, everyone around him was doing it. He repeated the action of searching over and over again every day, and he got a rush every time he found something good. Steve unwittingly followed the golden rule of habits: The easier you make it to put them on repeat (and the harder you make repeating the habits you want to lose), the more success you'll have.

This is why scheduling new habits first thing in the morning often gets you the best results: It's easier to do things before the distractions of the day worm their way into your progress. This is also why who and what you surround yourself with is so crucial: It's easier to quit drinking soda if you surround yourself with people who don't drink it and if you never keep any in your house; it's easier to go to yoga if the studio's just down the street; it's easier to be successful if you hang out with inspiring, successful people; it's easier to stop watching TV if you keep it in the garage; it's easier to have a negative outlook on marriage if you're raised by divorced, unhappy people; it's easier to accept fish as a breakfast food if you live in Japan.

5. **Patience.** Most habits score woefully low in the immediate gratification department. With the exception of things like taking a shower (instant clean and refreshed body!), making your bed (my room's suddenly so tidy!), or eating breakfast (I'm not hungry anymore!), most habits take awhile to produce the desired result, which makes them more difficult to stick with because we humans love us some payoff. Eating lentils instead of ice cream will eventually, hopefully, help lower your cholesterol; lifting weights every day may or may not take forever to produce a tight ab or the swell of a new muscle; meditating for thirty minutes a day may one day make you instantly feel more calm and centered, but first it may leave you wondering what the hell the point is for years. This is why things like relishing the fact that you're showing up at all is so important, why keeping track of the progress you've made so you can see how far you've come is so helpful, why looking for the little victories and rewards is so encouraging (*I want to die after the fiftieth*

*sit-up, but I used to want to die after the thirtieth—
woot!).*

Anchoring in a habit is like moving a giant pile of pebbles from one place to another, stone by stone: You make a tiny dent, hone your moves, it gets easier and easier every time you do it, and eventually you will indeed be staring at a new pile of rocks. You just can't always see your progress as it's happening.

Later in the book I'm going to give you tips that'll help you practice patience and stay the course while your habit takes its own sweet time to settle in, but right now I want to go deeply into the most important tip for creating a new habit—and for making any major upgrade in your life, really:

> Shift your identity to match the
> habits you're adopting.

6. **Identity.** Studies have shown that nearly half of the actions we perform every day are habitual: drinking a cup of morning coffee, praying, slouching, bitching, talking with our mouths full, looking for shiny things on the

ground, etc. But habits are responsible for much more than just the actions we take. Our beliefs, thoughts, and words are also habits, habits that inform the way we perceive the world around us, mold our identities, and, yes, take the actions we take.

One of the main reasons we fail to stick to new good habits and ditch negative ones is that we focus on changing what we're doing (or not doing) without also making sure that we embrace this habit as a new and valuable part of our identity. For example, if you decide you're going to lose thirty pounds, along with refraining from eating a bunch of crap, filling your fridge with healthy, low-cal food, working out, and getting a tattoo that says *If it's fried, it's denied*, you also need to become the person who weighs thirty pounds less, who struts around like, *Yeah, this is my body, these are my excellent eating habits; it's no biggie, it's just who I am and how I roll*. If you're identifying instead as the heavier version of yourself who somehow miraculously dropped thirty pounds, you'll most likely put the weight back on because you're still identifying as someone who has a weight issue. It's why people who win the lottery almost always wind up broke again—they still identify as broke (*Me? Rolling in the dough? Who would have ever thunk it? I keep waiting to wake up and wind up back in my normal life, this amount of money doesn't even seem real,* etc.) even though they've suddenly become rich.

In Alcoholics Anonymous, along with laying off the booze, refraining from hanging out in bars, and calling your sponsor whenever you feel yourself slipping, you're also asked to anchor in your identity every time you speak at a meeting: "Hi, I'm Janice, and I'm an alcoholic." By owning the fact that you're an addict and, hence, cannot and will not touch a drop of alcohol, you're much more likely to successfully dump your drinking habit than if you identified yourself this way: "Hi, I'm Janice, and even though I wake up hungover and unsure of where I am on a regular basis, I can handle the random cocktail here and there, no problemo." By shifting your identity to align with the habits you're working to adopt, you prepare yourself to live in a totally new reality by erasing the inner struggle of *I'm doing X but I'm actually an impostor so it probably won't last because it's not really who I am.*

> Changing your actions in order to form a new habit without also changing who you're being is like running into the wind: Yes, it's possible to put your head down, run as hard as you can, and gain some ground, but you're much more likely to give up and return to your old ways than if you run in the same direction as the wind.

Getting a handle on how you perceive yourself and the world around you is critical because of a certain driving force that all but the most highly evolved humans fall prey to on a daily basis: the human need to be right. There are few things that make the human heart sing more than getting every answer right on a test; than discovering that I, and not my friend who kept me waiting for an hour, wrote down the correct time to meet; than correctly guessing that Jill and Rob would be pregnant within the year; than having your chosen candidate sweep the election; than knowing Nirvana was cool before everyone else figured it out. We literally kill one another because we righteously believe this land is my land, not your land, that you should govern, worship, love, appear, and generally just behave the way that I deem is the correct way. We're so in love with being right we even gather in groups and swap stories of our proudest, most rightest moments: "I told Sheila that if she stands up in the canoe, she's going to fall in. So what does she do? She stands up in the canoe. And what happens? Mmmm-hmmm."

> There are three little words that all humans long to hear more than any others: You. Are. Right.

Our need to prove that our version of reality is real and right goes way beyond our fragile egos' need for validation, however, and often touches on something much more primal.

Here's how our deep, down-and-dirty need to be right works:

- **Human being + being right = I am safe.** Subconsciously, I need to know that X is true because it has formed my perception of reality. Having a reality that is solid means I feel secure in spite of the fact that I'm spinning around on a ball in infinite space, and that my impending death is actually the only thing I can be absolutely sure of.

- **Human beings are scared shitless of change.** Change dismantles the "known" and pulls our sense of security out from under us. Change opens up a never-before-experienced void of possibility *that could actually be, and oftentimes is, way more awesome than the known experience we're clinging to.* BUT, because change is unknown and threatens our reality, it makes us very uncomfy, so we tend to take great precautions to stay as far away from it as possible. Even the most daredevily among us have their limits (although, erm, they may not easily admit it). If you're a person who prides yourself on being a great adventurer, who's up for anything, who claims to embrace change—*I freakin' spoon change to sleep every night, m'kay?*—dig deep and own up to the excuses you fall back on when a particular change is out of your comfort zone. Also realize that there could be changes you've never even considered that could totally blindside you (losing all your money, having your house float away in a flood, finding out that your mom is a serial killer). There ain't no shame in being human, and owning your fears is essential if you want to move through them.

- **Human beings would often rather adapt to the fun-free familiar instead of risking the unknown.** Until (and unless) the familiar becomes so unbearable that they're willing to risk taking the leap into the void of change.

Because of our hell-bent dedication to being right, when it comes to our favorite topic—ourselves—we will defend our identities to the death *even if we're miserable and our identities aren't something we're proud of.* For example, back in the day, when I was perfecting the art of being perpetually broke, I would get extremely grouchy if anyone questioned my ability to be financially successful, because it threatened the rickety identity I was familiar with. *What do you mean I could make money if I changed my attitude and did things differently? I've tried for FORTY YEARS to make money as a writer and I'm living in a garage, cutting my own hair, and sleeping on a futon on the floor. I suck at making money. Trust me, I have a lifetime of proof.*

Even if we'd love to make a change, we subconsciously fear that if we stop believing our stories about who we are and what's available to us, the foundation of our realities will disappear and we will disappear right along with it. A tad dramatic, yes, but powerful enough to inspire people to spend entire lifetimes stuck in jobs they hate and abysmal relationships and to generally deny themselves the things and experiences that would have them leaping out of bed in toe-stubbing excitement each morning.

We are constantly, whether we realize it or not, building a case for our rightness. When I was broke and living in the garage, I was always on the lookout for proof that I couldn't make money: I spat on the ground about all the evil things people did to make and keep their money so I could prove that the quest for riches was amoral (as opposed to acknowledging all the beautiful things people did for and with money). I surrounded myself with other broke people who gave me tips on the best credit cards to transfer my debts to, who told me where the good thrift stores were, and who loved to bitch and moan about how expensive everything was too (as opposed to people who would kick my ass to up my game). I was a master at finding fire sales, the cheapest gas stations in town, and roadblocks to my success (as opposed to terrifying/exciting/lucrative opportunities that pushed me to grow and totally change my life for the better).

> Our "realities" are determined by how we habitually perceive ourselves and our worlds.

In every single moment there is an infinite number of ideas, sights, sounds, smells, opinions, and opportunities swirling around us, and what we choose to focus our attention on, and how we choose to think and speak about it, is based on the reality we're participating in at the moment. For example, four people can walk by a woman standing on a ladder, painting the outside of her house, and each person can experience this a completely different way. Let's say one of the people walking by is newly engaged, and when she looks at the woman she feels all fluttery and thinks, *I can't wait to pick out a color to paint our new house together!* Let's say the second person walking by just got cheated on by yet another in a long line of terrible girlfriends. He may look at the woman, find her attractive, but then think, *Don't fall for it, man, she'll rope you in and then toss you out like an old rag.* And let's say the third person walking by is launching a business as a shoe designer. She may look at the woman and think, *That's such an interesting place to put a buckle on a sandal. I wonder where she got those.* The last person, a busy mother of three who skipped breakfast, might glance at the woman and think, *Maybe I'll have a roast beef sandwich for lunch.*

The first step to making any major change in your life is always awareness. When it comes to matching your identity to the habits you want to form or free yourself from, you're going to want to start noticing the specifics of how you're behaving right now so you can change anything that's not in alignment with where you're heading. Pay attention to your words, thoughts, beliefs, and actions, and challenge yourself with thoughts like *Hmm, if I want to be a nonsmoker, maybe I shouldn't beg my boyfriend to roll down his window when we drive by someone smoking a cigarette so I can savor the secondhand smoke. Perhaps I should ignore that person and simply ask my boyfriend how his day was.*

> Identities come equipped
> with matching habits.

When I finally decided that I was going to heal my relationship with money (as in: go out and actually make some), I did everything I could think of to crawl out of my hole—I read books about wealth consciousness, went to money-making seminars, took classes, hired coaches— but one of the most profound things I did was change who I was being. I forced myself to stop identifying as a broke-ass loser and to start identifying as someone who made money effortlessly. Nothing had changed yet in my environment or my bank account, but I acted as if it had. I started thinking, acting, and perceiving the world like the person I wanted to become. For example, every time

I had the impulse to say *I can't afford it* (which was pretty much anytime anyone asked me to do anything), I'd replace it with this thought: *Money flows to me easily and freely*. I walked around saying this to myself all day long, and because I am human and I love to be right, I started looking for proof that money did indeed flow to me easily and freely. I'd find a dollar on the street, I'd get a freelance job out of nowhere, I'd get twenty bucks from Dad for my birthday—and instead of ignoring these tiny moments of financial felicity or immediately falling back into focusing on what the hell I was doing with my life, I celebrated that money was right then and there flowing to me easily and freely.

> Habits define who you're being
> at a certain moment in time; they're
> not who you are.

Not only did putting *Money flows to me easily and freely* on repeat make me feel a whole lot more inspired but it opened my eyes to all the things I couldn't see when I was so busy proving that *I can't afford it* was the truth. I went after opportunities that before would have been "out of my reach" or full-on invisible to me; I invested money "I didn't have" on educating myself and starting a new business; I stretched myself and took terrifying leaps into the unknown instead of hiding in the snore-hole of whining and complaining about how hard everything was. Adopting the identity of someone who was successful made me look for solutions, whereas identifying as someone who was broke made me look for excuses. It was large, Marge.

> "I am the greatest. I said that even before I knew I was." —Muhammad Ali

Pick an identity right now that you've often used to describe yourself—it can be anything from being lazy to organized to punctual to spontaneous to confident to musical to bad at math to a real people pleaser. We're going to step back and notice how your habitual words, thoughts, beliefs, feelings, and actions have helped you form this identity, so that when you work on developing new identities and new habits, you have an example from your own life to use as a reference.

- **Words:** How do you talk about yourself in reference to this identity of yours? Do you apologize for it? Celebrate it? Act like it's no big deal? For example,

I'm an extremely tidy person. I make my bed the moment I get up in the morning, immediately unpack and put away my stuff when I get home from a trip, and put my spices away while I'm still cooking even though I almost always need to get them out and use them again (grumbles at self). I also have a constant stream of houseguests and often find myself saying, "I know, I can't help it, just ignore me," while gently pushing them aside so I can fluff the pillow behind them or while neatly lining up all our shoes in the front hallway. I often make announcements to anyone who will listen, such as "I'm glad I'm so persnickety. It makes my life so much easier," as I pull my lipstick out of the pocket in my purse where it always is because I always put it back where it belongs. I like being tidy, I've always been tidy, I'm into it and my words reflect it.

- **Thoughts:** What thoughts run through your mind when you do things like walk into a room, meet a new person, read the news, or drive down a new street as a result of who you're being? For example, if I walk into someone's office and see a bunch of stuff piled on their desk, I get anxious and can't fathom how they're able to concentrate with all that crap all over the place. Clutter makes me think about cleaning. Tidiness makes me think all is well. I like tidiness in other people too. I notice right away when I walk into someone's house if stuff is put away or not.

- **Beliefs:** What beliefs, conscious or unconscious, are you buying into as a result of who you're being? Being tidy makes my life easier because I always know where my stuff is. I've got my own back. I have my act together. I'm in control.

- **Feelings:** When you think about being X, what comes up for you emotionally? Tidiness makes me feel calm, accomplished, happy, secure, safe, cozy, and a little superior to people who aren't tidy. There. I said it.

- **Repeated action:** What habitual actions do you find yourself repeating because of who you're being? For me, it's straightening, fluffing, folding, stacking, sponging off, organizing, repeatedly walking into rooms I've just tidied up to revel in how great they look.

Now that you're aware of the specifics that go into making up an identity, you are ready to use this information to create excellent new habits and toss out lousy old ones. The ability to choose and change who we're being in this life is a gift, especially since so many of the habits and identities that we're walking around with weren't consciously chosen by us in the first place. Science has shown that we're genetically predisposed toward certain personality traits, and our environment also influences the behaviors and beliefs we cling to. We picked up the majority of our most ingrained and habitual beliefs and identities from our parents (or from whoever raised us). We didn't, as four-year-olds, think, *Well, I agree, it seems like an excellent idea to be disdainful of anyone who doesn't share the same religious beliefs as I do. Disliking people who are different is totally aligned with what I find fun and nourishing and meaningful—I'm in.* When it comes to most of our early habits, we kinda just pick them up while hanging around the dinner table and watching every single move our parents make. Then we go ahead and form our own versions of the truth in one of two ways: by mimicking what we take in or by rebelling against it.

When you were a kid, the people who raised you were the centers of your universe. You relied on them to keep you safe, to get you food, and to show you the ropes of this big new world of yours. You were like a little mouse, nibbling up every morsel of information you could get your paws on. As a child, you hadn't developed any filters or analytical skills yet, so you basically just internalized and categorized all this intel with a big, awkward Yes/No switch, and either copied or did the opposite of what you saw around you.

What you lacked in analytical prowess, however, you made up for in detail. My brother Stephen discovered just how astutely he'd absorbed all the info from our parents when, as an adult, he accidentally caught himself on video making sandwiches and hors d'oeuvres while standing next to our dad. It was his daughter's eighteenth birthday, and we were all at his house for her surprise party. Steve set up a camera on the kitchen counter and pointed it toward the door so he could capture the big moment when she walked into the house. What he didn't realize was that he was also capturing himself and Dad, so when he asked me over the next morning to show me the footage, he prefaced it with "I had no idea. Why didn't anybody tell me? I had no idea." He cued up the incriminating footage, and there they were, Dad and Steve standing side by side at the counter, Big Me and Mini Me with the exact same posture: shoulders up, head bent slightly forward with a little jovial shake here and there, arms a little stiff, holding their respective knives with the exact same fingers in the exact same position, cutting with the same precise concentration, raising the same right eyebrow while listening intently to the conversation around them. Steve not only set the camera up perfectly—Dad in the foreground, his antipasto-plate-preparing stunt double slightly off to his right—he couldn't have imitated Dad better if he'd tried. It was the most flawless and impressive performance I've ever seen.

There's no fighting it; we become our parents whether we like it or not. I don't know about you, but I sometimes hear my mother's words come flying out of my mouth with such hair-raising precision it's like she's hiding behind a bush feeding me lines. I even find myself saying things I picked up from her that I don't necessarily agree with or want to say, but lo and behold, they come blurting out of my mouth by habit, like coughed-up hairballs from my unconscious.

Sometimes, though, we rebel against our early conditioning, and we reject what we've taken in with the same dedicated attention to detail that we employ when we're mimicking. I credit my extreme tidiness to the fact that my mom was an avid stuff enthusiast: Surrounding herself with clutter gave her a sense of security, perhaps filling some hole from her lonely childhood. Mom was of the mind that if you found a shirt you liked, you should buy it in every color; she had about thirty-seven baseball caps fighting for space on the hooks in her coatroom; papers, magazines, spare dog collars, and emery boards teetered in piles on every available surface. One time when I was home from college, I discovered a stockpile of old moisturizer bottles in her attic, all with less than half a container left and all of them dating back to somewhere around 1970. I asked her if I could throw them away, to which she replied, "No." To which I replied, "Why on Earth are you keeping them?" To which she replied, "Why on Earth do you care?" Fair enough. Her attic, her crusty lotion. But to me, that kind of clutter is the opposite of comforting; to me, it's a sinister evil that's intent on unraveling the very fibers that hold together my soul. I became so traumatized by her collecting that I developed the opposite identity, honing a tidiness that has become so legendary that it once inspired a houseguest to wake up screaming in the middle of the night after realizing with a start that she'd left a dirty spoon on my spotless kitchen counter.

Living an awesome life is all about making choices that make your heart sing, and in order to do this, you must become aware of the choices you've already made.

> Trying to change your life without being self-aware is like using a map to try to get somewhere you've never been before: If you don't know where you're starting from, you ain't gonna get very far.

Pulling back and taking stock of your habits, your beliefs, your thoughts, your identity, your words, and your actions is some of the most important work you can do, because it gets you out of victim mode and puts you in control of your life. And living a life on purpose is truly where the party's at.

GAVE UP REFINED SUGAR, ALICE, 32

The impulse to give up sugar was mostly about my skin. I would get terrible breakouts and generally didn't feel well after I ate it. When I do something, my approach is to go balls to the wall—I made a big announcement, out loud, "I'm quitting sugar," and got rid of all the sugary products in my house. I did a lot of research on people who changed their lives through food, I worked alongside a doctor who was very inspirational to me, and I watched a really interesting documentary called *Fed Up* that demonized sugar.

I also did something I call *tweaking the addiction*. I realized that I was addicted to eating sugar and lots of garbage to reinforce how bad I felt about myself. Once I distanced myself a little bit from sugar so it wasn't habitual anymore, I was able to see how sugar was coloring my life: I was very up and down emotionally, my skin would break out, and I was like, *Why am I doing this to myself?* So then I started to align myself with food that made me feel really good and I broke the addiction to feeling bad.

> When you're not addicted to feeling bad about
> yourself anymore, you change your habits.

So instead I tweaked my addiction to feeling bad about myself and became addicted to feeling good in general and good about myself.

I also got into a character like I was in a play. I connected with images and internalized stories that represented me at my best, truest self: I am not a person who eats sugar. I changed my story; it's very method acting and very helpful. Because if you don't think that you are something, how can you partake in the behavior associated with it?

CHAPTER 2

HEALTHY BOUNDARIES:
THE UNSUNG HEROES OF
SUCCESSFUL HABITS

I grew up in a suburban neighborhood that was teeming with kids more or less my own age. We had trees to climb, woods to build forts in, backyards with swing sets, and a steep incline at the top of our street that was excellent for riding a bike or a skateboard down at alarmingly high speeds.

One late summer afternoon when I was about five years old, a bunch of us were outside playing when Charles, my four-year-old next-door neighbor, decided to ride his bike down the hill all on his own and see how fast he could go. I don't remember watching him walk to the top of the street or seeing him come down the hill; what I do remember is the part where his tire hit a rock, his bike flew out from under him, and he traveled a good six feet along the road on his face. Everything after that happened in slow motion: all of us kids screaming and running up the road toward our fallen friend; Charles peeling himself off the ground, his face slowly erupting into a bloody, slobbery howl; and our babysitter, Janet, probably only thirteen herself, with her skinny arms flailing all over the place, grabbing Charles and yelling, "Jennifer! Go get his parents!"

The parents were all at a cocktail party down the street at the Hayneses' house, gathered together on their giant screened-in porch, sipping gin and tonics and luxuriating in their temporarily child-free status. I ran all the way there but slowed to an unenthusiastic stroll as I approached the house, realizing with terror that I was about to walk into a roomful of adults. I made my way around the side of the house to the dreaded porch, fully hidden from view thanks to the fact that it sat high off the ground. Peeking inside, all I could see was a sea of legs, so many legs of so many grown-ups who would all stop talking and stare at me when I climbed up the three big concrete steps, made my surprise entrance, and stam-

mered out my news. I was terrified of being in the spot-
light, terrified of getting in trouble for playing in the
street, terrified of grown-ups in general, so I reached up
from my hiding place next to the steps and knocked ever
so inaudibly on the very bottom corner of the screen
door. Then I turned and ran all the way to my house, got
into my bed, and tried to conjure up the stomachache
that I was prepared to fake the second my parents got
home.

This is how many of us deal with setting certain boundaries: When it comes to getting clear on, and standing up
for, who we are and what we need, we timidly knock on
the door, if we even show up to knock at all. Then we
slink off and curl up into a ball of our self-imposed suffering. Like a little kid who's scared of getting scolded or
who doesn't want to upset anyone or who's just generally
afraid of being seen, singled out, or judged, we opt for
*No, that's fine, ignore this gigantic stack of work on my desk,
what can I do for you?* and leave our own needs lying in the
street, crying out for help. (Charles ended up being fine
and still speaks to me, btw.)

Personal boundaries define where you end and the outside world begins. Having healthy boundaries means owning your actions, emotions, and needs as well as *not* owning
the actions, emotions, and needs of others.

> You are responsible *to* other people.
> You are not responsible *for* other
> people. Big diff.

Just as our skin is the boundary that defines our physical bodies, the walls of our homes define our living spaces, and fifteen items or less at the grocery store means fifteen items, people, not twenty, we have personal boundaries that need to be clearly defined and respected as well. For example, we need to be able to decline invitations we don't want to accept, to confront people who make comments that cause us discomfort, and to tell our boss to stop parking in our parking spot already. We need to ask for help when we need it, to lose the expectation that other people will fix our problems, and to quit bailing out our financially irresponsible sister every time she goes on a shopping bender and can't afford her rent. If we don't set our own clear and healthy boundaries, we spill out and become messy, murky blobs, intertwining our needs, roles, and identities with those of the people around us.

Healthy boundaries are especially critical when it comes to creating new habits, because in order to stay the course, you can't afford to have your time structured by outside forces, your beliefs swayed by naysayers, or your attention consumed by your (often unconscious) need to control those around you. Your guilt, shame, and shoulds cannot run the show.

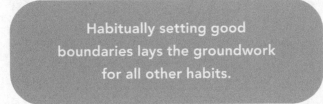

Habitually setting good boundaries lays the groundwork for all other habits.

If you're developing the habit of becoming a better manager at work, for example, you need to create solid boundaries by articulating your expectations, laying down clear guidelines, allowing your employees the space to flourish without hovering over them and micromanaging, and being neither a friend nor a tyrant to those you manage. If you're getting into the habit of not eating meat, you need to ask your friends to meet at restaurants with good vegetarian options, take time to learn new, meat-free recipes, and inform unamused dinner party hosts that you don't eat animals. If you're going to regularly do Tai Chi, you need to give yourself all the time you need to honor your practice, you need to surround yourself with encouraging people to develop the dedication to keep showing up, and you need to focus on yourself and your craft so you can move in slow motion without falling over (or asleep).

> Your habits define who you're being.
> Your boundaries define the space
> you require in order to be
> who you're being.

To help you up your game with your new habit, take a minute to think about how well you respect—and whether or not you're even aware of—your own boundaries and the limits that other people set. Here are some common areas where boundaries come into play and some examples to help spark self-reflection:

- **The bod:** If you don't like being touched by strangers and a yoga teacher comes over to adjust your pose, do you ask her to please stop, do you move away, do you slap her on the wrist, or do you say nothing and hope she backs off soon? What are your boundaries when it comes to sex, the food you eat, the exercise you do, the clothes you wear, and the conversations you have about your body and about bodies in general? How do you respond to people who say hello by kissing you on the lips (are you one of them)? How aware are you of other people's body language? Do you automatically go in for the hug when you meet someone or do you tune into what they're up for first? Do you raise a disapproving eyebrow when your daughter, whom you consider to be overweight, helps herself to a second donut? Do you encourage her to eat the donut? Do you make fun of her? Do you leave her alone? Do you notice?

- **Stuff:** Which of your possessions are off-limits to others and which do you share freely? Are you tidy or messy in your own home, and how do you behave in the homes of others? Do you live by the old adage *Ask for forgiveness, not for permission*, and help yourself to the apples on your neighbor's apple tree, the clothes in your sister's closet, office supplies from the storage room at work, or your spouse's toothbrush when you accidentally leave yours behind on a trip? How would you respond, if at all, if the tables were turned and people didn't ask for permission from you?

- **Beliefs:** Are your beliefs easily swayed by the beliefs of the people around you or by the media? Are you fairly solid in your beliefs yet still open to hearing another point of view? Do you think people who disagree with you are morons or that they're smarter than you or that they're just different from you? Do you question your beliefs or the beliefs of others? Is it important to you that in every confrontation someone is right and someone is wrong, or can you hold space for the possibility that there may be more than one right answer? Will you fight to the death to be right about the fact that it was your husband, not you, who left the car window open in the rainstorm last week (even though, erm, you're actually not so sure it wasn't you now that you think about it)? Can you admit when you're wrong? Do you need everyone within shouting distance to know you were right when you're right? Do you refuse to hear anyone out and never consider the other side of things? Does anyone actually admit to any of this?

• **Behavior:** Do you go with the flow and behave however you feel in the moment, oblivious to how it affects others? Do you limit your behavior, constantly apologize, shrink down, and speak in a barely audible whisper so as not to make waves or disturb others? Do you take a stand if someone is being inconsiderate, bullying, making racist jokes, or talking loudly during a movie, or do you stay silent or complain about them behind their backs? Do you foist unsolicited ideas, books, fashion suggestions, job opportunities, and blind dates on others because you see such potential in them? How do you respond, if at all, to unsolicited advice, rude remarks, a helping hand? Do you try to do everything yourself? Do you try to get others to do everything for you? Do you blame other people/society/ your parents for your boring job, your terrible taste in partners, your empty bank account, your fear of flying? Do you communicate clearly, drop hints, think before you speak, blurt it out, or hold it in until you explode/grow a tumor?

- **Space:** Are you a bed hog or a road hog, do you sit with your legs spread wide apart on a crowded subway? What do you do, if anything, when confronted with people who are and do? Do you sit with barely even one cheek on the couch to take up less room? Are you aware of the space you take up? Do you give yourself and others room to work, room to think, room to create, room to feel? Do you guard your privacy and respect the privacy of others?

- **Emotions:** Do you empathize with others, over-empathize with others and take on their pain as your own, or do you feel nothing when it ain't your problem? Do you have screaming matches in airports with the ticket agent who can't find your reservation, do you calmly discuss the problem, or do your burst into tears of frustration? Do you bottle up your feelings, share them with only those closest to you, or try not to feel them at all? Do you act impulsively on how you feel or let your emotions run their course before making a decision, and how do you respond, if at all, to people who process differently than you do? Do you adjust your behavior if someone around you is in a bad mood, a good mood, a sad mood, and/or do you expect everyone to meet you where you're at emotionally? Are you aware of other people's moods? Do you try to fix other people's bad moods?

- **Time:** Do you respect your time and others' by being punctual? Do you refuse to suffer those who waste your time? Do you take the time to read your neighbor's entire book about the local flora and fauna against your will, or do you tell her you're too busy? Do you take guilt-free alone time for yourself? Do you complain that you can't find the time to do what you want to do, do you make time, do you waste time?

- **Availability:** Do you make yourself available for intimacy, friendship, success, fun? Do you make yourself available for verbal abuse, negative energy, toxic relationships, the unappealing whims of others? Do you listen to your friend complain about her job for the five hundredth time or do you tell her you can't hear it anymore and to get her act together/tell it to someone else? Do you let people you don't like into your life/home/book group because you don't want them to feel bad/make a scene? Are you more available for the needs of others than for your own needs? Are you aware of the needs of others?

- **Energy:** Do you eat food, listen to music, participate in activities, hang out with people who give you energy or deplete your energy? Do you disengage from people and activities that drain you, or do you suck it up and power through or find some "happy" medium? Do you pay attention to who and what affects your energy? What do you bring to the party in the energy department?

We first learn about boundaries as children. We test the waters with the people around us, see how it goes, and base our understanding of how things are after years of studying the results we witness. If we say no to giving Aunt Lauren a kiss, are our wishes heard and respected, do we get ignored and lifted up to her cheek for a smooch against our will, or do we get punished and sent to our rooms? When we do what we're told and go get ready for bed, are we rewarded with a story, do we get yelled at for taking too long, or are we left upstairs by ourselves for hours? When we test out the new snappy comeback we learned from the big kids on the bus and call Mom a fucking bitch next time she asks us to clean up our toys, we gain all sorts of valuable information from her response (even though we still may have no idea what the hell we just said).

Our little brains take in all the information we get and then form "truths" about which boundaries will best protect us and get us what we need. *I'm treated like a bad, mean person when I say no, so I'm never gonna say that again,* or *Dad is always angry and tired when he comes home from work, so being quiet, needing nothing, and not being seen is the way to avoid getting yelled at.* We may then go on to spend the rest of our lives suffering from the bad boundaries we formed based on these outdated "truths." We don't realize that what we've assumed to be simple facts of life are actually just perceptions of reality formed through our own experiences, and that many of these experiences took place during a time when we hadn't yet learned to speak in full sentences and thought that sticking peas up our nose was a great idea.

Luckily, there's another option, one in which we wake up and realize that we can choose to question our beliefs rather than spend our lives blindly playing victim to the ones that no longer work for us. *I'm always the one in our group of friends who organizes dinner parties, plans camping trips, gets tickets to concerts, navigates cancellations, rearranges things when people's schedules change, and guess what? I'm exhausted. And grouchy. I caught myself fantasizing about collapsing in Costco, being hauled out on a stretcher, and everybody having to take care of me for a change. Shouldn't I be fantasizing about lying on a beach somewhere, mainlining snacks? Why do I feel like if I ask for help I'm a bad person? Is that true?* As we move through life and uncover these cranky old "truths," we can unhook ourselves from them, shift our focus onto beliefs that support who we're becoming, and empower ourselves to create the boundaries we need to grow: *Denying my needs is a drag. I'm going to stop acting like I'll be punished by Daddy for speaking up, stop pretending I can do everything myself, and ask for some damn help around here.*

> What we choose to believe is true or not true dictates the boundaries we do or don't set.

Whether or not we're aware of it, we're always making choices about setting healthy boundaries, setting unhealthy boundaries, or setting no boundaries at all. Depending on our upbringing, how evolved we are, the situation, and how many cocktails we've had, we either stand up for our needs and the needs of others or we throw our and everyone else's needs under the bus.

We've all got countless cringeworthy stories and creative ways in which we've dropped the ball, but for the most part, our boundary issues fall into one of three categories.

THE THREE COMMON TYPES OF BOUNDARY BUNGLE-RY

1. Too yessy.

   We say yes to everything because we want to avoid confrontations, disappointing others, appearing selfish, or missing out on the chance to feel needed and important.

2. Too much no.

   We say no to everything for fear of being seen, disappointed, disappointing, judged, inadequate, needy, or hurt. We put up a wall to hide behind as opposed to creating a boundary that allows us to fully flourish.

3. Too controlly.

We try to control other people, get them to take on our problems, and/or become overly involved with their problems. We seek out those who will enable us and/or become enablers ourselves because we don't want to fix our own lives; we want to feel in control, needed, loved, and not alone.

Most of us participate in a bit of all of these behaviors to some degree, depending on our issues, the circumstances, and who happens to be the lucky navigator of our bad boundaries at the moment. For example, we may say yes to all of the things that our boss asks us to do that are outside our job description, to the point of exhaustion and resentment; we may say no to invitations to parties and blind dates to avoid awkwardness and rejection; and we may be controlly with our kids by getting involved in areas of their lives that are none of our business: "I got rid of those black clunky boots that you've worn to death and got you something a little more . . . feminine."

> One of the premier causes
> of unnecessary drama is
> bad boundaries.

Having bad boundaries doesn't make us bad people, it just makes us regular ol' people who are trying to avoid feeling pain and isolation by behaving in ways that ultimately cause us to feel the very pain and isolation we're trying to avoid—joke's on us! The excellent news is that you simply need to become aware of where and when your boundaries aren't so great, make the conscious decision to upgrade them *regardless of how uncomfortable and/or scary it may be*, and take back some control of your own life. Take back some control—ain't nobody ever gonna be perfect or completely in control of anything, but we can certainly improve the quality of our lives by getting better at making smarter choices.

Here's where we get confused when it comes to boundaries: we want to be nice, to bring joy to others, to be good, helpful, agreeable, compassionate, popular people—and we think that compromising our boundaries is the best way to meet the most needs. We mistakenly perceive boundaries to be bad, mean, unbending barriers that keep others out. We fear that setting a boundary means we're cutting ourselves off from others, delivering an ultimatum, putting up a wall, being demanding, controlling, rigid, and worst of all, selfish. Meanwhile, clearly defining who you are and what you're available for isn't selfish but rather it's self-ish. For example, telling your teenagers that they're unauthorized to disturb you unless it involves the police during the thirty minutes you've set aside to read and meditate every afternoon is indeed self-serving, but it also benefits your kids. By setting a boundary and taking time for yourself, your children not only get a more relaxed, attentive mother who values herself but also an excellent model for how to set good boundaries themselves and much-needed practice respecting the boundaries of others.

Think about what a relief it is when someone tells you exactly what's on their mind, what they need, and what they're available for. Even if the boundary they set isn't the most convenient or beneficial to your own needs, knowing where they stand beats the hell out of trying to read their mind, walking around on eggshells, or trying to figure out if their evening performance of slamming drawers and silently moving their mashed potatoes around on their plate is about something you did or said or if it's even about you at all.

> Good, clear boundaries are a gift to everyone. Resentment, exhaustion, guilt, obligation, and passive-aggressiveness are gifts to no one.

The problem is that, quite often, when we bravely take a stand and declare that we are no longer available to make dinner every night of the week because we now have choir practice, people don't exactly pick up quickly on the gift aspect of the new boundary we've set. Especially the people we care the most about. Over the course of the nearly ten years that I've been speaking on the topic of badassery, rarely do I get through a Q&A without this question rearing its head: *What do you do when the people closest to you don't support who you're becoming?*

The reason this question is so common is that when you change who you're being—which involves developing new habits and boundaries—your transformation often upsets those closest to you because:

1. **They no longer get to be right about who you're being,** and, as we know, since they are human, they love to be right. If and when they understand and accept the new you, they get to be right again and will feel better

about the whole thing. If they never understand and accept the new you, they will act out (see below).

2. **You've gone from a known entity to a new, unknown entity, and people fear the unknown with the same zest they have for being right.** On a primal level, the new you changes an aspect of their "reality," and if what they perceived to be real is now not real, it's upsetting. It also suggests that more things about their reality could slip away—*If my best drinking buddy no longer drinks and has a boundary about no booze being allowed in her house, what, dear God, what other things that I rely on are going to disappear?*

3. **You're showing them that change is possible.** You're basically giving them unsolicited advice simply by being—*If I can better myself, so can you.* If they're not available to receive this information, if they'd prefer to cling to the familiar things in their lives that aren't bringing them a whole lot of joy instead of making the changes they know they need to make, they're going to be grouchy, and perhaps snarky, around the new you.

4. **In order to shift who you're being and own the new you, you have to basically kill off your old identity, and people get unpleasant when you kill the people they love.** This is why, should you decide to take your

job more seriously and start dressing more profession-
ally, Joe at the deli, whom you hardly know, will give you
a high five and a *Lookin' good!* when he sees you on
your lunch break, and the people who allegedly love
you—your spouse/parents/besty—might say things like
Look at you, Mr. Fancypants, you too good for us now?

5. **If you've been terrible at setting boundaries your
whole life and suddenly start sticking up for your fine
self** and your needs, some people will be disappointed,
knocked out of first place, deprived of their doormat/
servant/chef/chauffeur, and might whine, plead, call you
selfish, and explain that they will perish if you stop doing
everything for them.

> The people closest to you have the
> most to lose by losing you, so they are
> the most resistant to you changing.

To express their disappointment and fear (almost all of
which is happening on a subconscious level that they're
unaware of, btw), the people in your inner circle might
make fun of you, worry about you, list all the reasons

why your big plans won't work, tell you you're no fun anymore, and in extreme cases, stop speaking to you. There will, of course, also be people close to you who cheer you on and/or who get inspired to upgrade their own lives thanks to your fine example. But the likelihood of those you love having a big ol' freak-out bears noting because it's one of the main reasons we refuse to change the habits we want to change and set the boundaries we need to set in order to change them.

> Changing your habits and your boundaries takes courage, audacity, and a whole lot of self-love.

Because we're uninterested in denying ourselves the things and experiences that light us up, for fear of making others uncomfy, we're gonna get really good at setting boundaries.

In order to help you create excellent boundaries that benefit you, give your new habit the space it needs to take root, and help you connect more authentically with the people in your world, let's break down the Three Common Types of Boundary Bungle-ry:

1. **Too yessy + any kind of even gentle confrontation = saying yes when you want to say no.**

Constantly saying yes when you'd really love to say no is the most famous boundary problem. It's the way many people try to win love and acceptance, and it's especially common in women, thanks to the patriarchal society in which we're raised, which teaches us it's not ladylike to take a stand for ourselves and our needs or to put ourselves first. We're just gonna go ahead and say a hearty *hell no* and a *fuck you very much* to that memo from the patriarchy, m'kay? M'kay.

Here's what a yes-when-you-want-to-say-no boundary looks like:

Imagine you're out shopping with a friend and she's trying on a pile of dresses for a big work event. You've spent a couple hours with her already but need to get home because tonight your ex has the kids and it's the only night that you've got time to pick up a fabulous dinner, take a bath, give yourself a facial, unwind, and watch a movie. You've been fantasizing about your night alone because you've been taking care of your family and working your ass off all week, but you let your friend talk you into staying with her in spite of yourself (literally). She says things like *I helped you pick out a dress for your brother's wedding. You're so much better at knowing what looks good on me than I am. This event is really important to me. I really need you right now. It'll only take ten minutes, I swear.* She lays on a thick, gooey layer of guilt, and before you know it, you've taken on her need to have a shopping buddy instead of holding the space for your own need to get home and pamper yourself. Thanks to your bad boundaries, you wind up spending another hour or two at the store, get home, shove some food down your throat, and pass out, angry at her and angry at yourself, with woefully unexfoliated skin.

Meanwhile, you could have set a boundary, told her what a great time you had, that you can't wait to see which dress she winds up with, but that you have to get home early and that's what you're doing. Setting this boundary makes her feelings and reactions her responsibility, not yours. This boundary reminds you (and her, even if she can't admit it or recognize it) that it's her choice, and really none of your business, whether she chooses to be (1) disappointed and/or angry, (2) impressed and inspired by your clarity and dedication to self-care, (3) grateful for the time that she did get to hang out with you, or (4) some combination of the above.

Here are some of the best ways to turn your unwanted yes into a no when you need to:

- **Take stock of your needs.** Think about a new habit you'd like to bring into your life and get clear on some boundaries you need to put into place to support this habit. For example, if you're getting into the habit of recording a podcast about your favorite bands every week, you need time to do your research, get all the technical aspects rolling, perhaps hire a producer/tech person, set up a studio, and make the recording. The main new boundary you're going to have to put into place will most likely be around protecting your time, meaning you'll perhaps have to start saying no to some of the demands of your family—always doing the grocery shopping, being readily available to drive your kids to the mall, listening to your adorable yet long-winded husband's stories about Slushmouth Stan from work. You may also have to say no to your friends, opt out of a regular lunch date with the girls, or cut down on chatting on the phone.

  Then there are the boundaries you need to set for yourself, like saying no to wasting time on social media and looking at pictures of baby animals online and generally getting good at organizing your time better. You're also going to have to toss some nos at your self-sabotaging thoughts like *Who the hell am I to have a podcast and a voice?* You'll have to say no to your fears of sounding like an idiot in front of an online sea of strangers, no to worrying that no one will show up to be a guest on your show, and no to your fear that you'll give up on your podcast after the first few weeks.

You'll also have to say no to friends who suggest you interview their favorite (sucky) bands and no to sucky bands that want to be on your show.

Taking a moment to figure out ahead of time where the difficult nos are going to occur will help you be prepared instead of caught off guard when the need to say no shows up, which will help you stand your ground.

- **Deal with your fear.** Chances are excellent that some sort of fear will rear its head when you take stock of your needs and the nos they require; otherwise you most likely wouldn't have been yessing these nos all along. An excellent way to defuse your fear is to break it down. Get into the specifics of what your fear is—*I'm scared if I tell my friend Mary that I won't put her favorite pan flute band on my podcast, she'll get mad at me.* Then what? *Then I'll feel guilty.* Then what? *Then it'll be weird between* us. Then what? *Then I guess she'll eventually get over it or she won't.* Then what? *Then we'll either go back to being friends or she'll never speak to me again.* Then what? *Then, either way, I'll get back to living my life.* The exercise of dismantling your fear is almost always very anticlimactic. And usually kinda embarrassing, because you realize that if Mary gets over her disappointment, your fears are basically unfounded, and if she chooses never to speak to you again because you're making healthy choices about something that's ultimately none of her business and is honestly so not a big deal, she's not really the kind of person you want to be friends with anyway.

I also want to mention here that if you feel like your fears are too much for you to overcome, if they have real, debilitating power over you, get your butt into therapy. Some of our boundary issues run incredibly deep, and because you're not screwing around about this changing your life thing, if you're having trouble dealing with something that's holding you back, going to therapy is some of the most important work you can do.

- **Own your nos.** Saying yes when you want to say no is a habit like any other, so start identifying as someone who says no easily. See yourself as someone who takes a stand, as someone who values your own needs, as someone who is more scared of living an inauthentic life than getting yelled at.

> When you say no to the needs of others, you're being nice to yourself, not mean to them.

Yes, we all have to make compromises in our relationships, but there's a difference between compromising and constantly letting yourself down. You can take care of the people you love AND take care of yourself, and when you say yes all the time, you're leaving yourself in the dust (and often enabling their bad behavior). Good boundaries are all about self-love. Be the kind of person who loves yourself and who loves others, and you will find that saying no will start to make you feel powerful, not guilty.

- **Know who trips you up the most.** We all have people in our lives we have a hard time saying no to, even when we desperately want to. Get clear on the people who excel at winning arguments, laying on the guilt, tugging at your heart, and scaring the hell out of you, so you can brace yourself and have your firm, no-nonsense no at the ready when they push back.

- **Practice in a safe space.** Practice saying no to things that aren't terribly loaded for you. Say no to the lady at the perfume counter who wants to spray you, say no to your nosy neighbor next time she invites you over for cocktails and a complain sesh about the Campbells across the street, say no to helping the PTA with their annual fundraiser, say no to the saleslady who brings a stack of shirts to your dressing room that she thinks will look great on you. Just say no. It's fun! Extra points if you refrain from apologizing.

- **Learn the language of no.** Getting your no on is all about clarity, kindness, speed, consistency, and commitment. "No" is a simple, short word; it's not full of long, drawn-out explanations, justifications, apologies, emotions, excuses, and backpedaling.

  Here are some general rules to saying a real good no:

  - **Make it all about you, not them.** It's not *You need to talk on the phone way too much, I can't take it, who the hell has that kind of time,* but rather *I need to limit my phone time because I'm getting really busy, so I can only talk to you once a week.* Keep the emotion out of it; don't try to second-guess what they're thinking or worry that they'll get upset. You are responsible for your end of the conversation, and if they get upset, that's their work, not yours.

- **Use direct language that gets straight to the point,** such as *Please call before you come over. Thanks so much for coming to my party, but I'm going to bed now, so y'all need to skedaddle. I'm not comfortable hugging strangers, but it's nice to meet you.* And the classic *No thanks.* Powerful no-type phrases often begin with *I need X, I won't X, I can't X, I don't like X, I'm not going to X, I'd appreciate it if X.*

- **Give yourself a cushion.** Because you will be caught off guard sometimes, and because getting good at saying no is a new muscle that you're strengthening, if you're feeling nervous or flustered and a nice squishy yes seems like the easiest way out, whip out an *I can't decide right now* or a *Let me think about it* or *Let me check my schedule and get back to you.* Instead of expecting yourself to be the master of no right out of the gate, keep phrases like this at the ready to give yourself time to pause so you can break the habit of agreeing to stuff immediately in order to escape your discomfort.

2. Too much no + any concept or idea that makes you uncomfortable = saying no when it would serve you best to say yes.

My mom is hilarious. She is the type of person who can whittle a joke out of any situation, no matter how grim or heartwarming or dull it may be. For example, one stunning spring afternoon, Mom and I sat in my garden watching the birds twitter about, luxuriating in the warm breeze, enveloped in a miraculous sea of flowers in bloom. We sat in silent reverence, taking it all in, completely overcome by peace and beauty and gratitude, or so I thought, until Mom broke the spell with *I'd hate to be a bird. You have to build your house with your face.* Mom's full of doozies, but like many people, she also hides behind her humor to avoid pain and discomfort— she's always been swift at letting one rip when presented with a difficult conversation or when she's feeling something she no wanna feel.

Mom was raised by well-meaning yet rather hardcore WASPs who believed that showing emotions is to be avoided at all costs, but should you insist on letting one slip out, please, for God's sake, do it in the other room. Thanks to years of therapy and forcing my quivery little heart to open up, I've been able to stop participating in this family tradition of stonewalling my feelings. Yet that being said, I'm no Olympian. I mean, I have friends who, in the middle of a crisis or a meltdown, *pick up the phone and call me*, sobbing so uncontrollably that they're barely able to breathe or speak as I stand on the other end of the phone, instantly frozen and dumbfounded, more shocked than if they'd shown up at my front door sporting nothing but a ponytail. These friends almost always call back, apologetic and embarrassed, but to me, this kind of vulnerability is staggering, courageous, highly advanced.

In other words, if you've got a knack for the no, if you go it alone at all costs instead of reaching out for the help you need, I feel you.

When we err on the side of saying no instead of yes, we're scared we'll push people away by letting them see what we consider to be our weak, broken, needy, burdensome sides. We don't want to risk being devastated by asking for love and getting rejected. We don't want to risk opening ourselves up to ridicule or finding ourselves smothered by other people's needs. We prefer to "play it safe," to remain in control by keeping a tight grip on our emotions, our surroundings, and our hearts. We build walls out of *I'm good, I got it, I'm fine*, as we carry an elephant, metaphorical and/or literal, up a staircase by ourselves.

> Boundaries are not rigid walls. They breathe and move with the complexities of life and the nuances of each situation.

It took me forever to hire an assistant, a COO, and a bookkeeper for my business, even once I had money coming in, because I was fully entrenched in the habit of doing everything myself and I didn't want to surrender control. I've also moved entire roomfuls of furniture by myself and once helped some friends plant their garden the day after breaking up with my boyfriend, opting to run to the bathroom and furtively sob and pretend I was grappling with a cold instead of letting them know I was unraveling. Getting older has worked wonders for my boundary-setting prowess, and ever since hitting fifty I've noticed that saying *yes, no, sounds like you've got a problem there, get the hell off my lawn*—whatever the situation calls for—comes to me much more easily. My dad, who lived to be ninety-two, said it best: *I don't know if you get older and wiser or older and just more tired.* I think it's a bit of both: As we age, we (hopefully) gain wisdom through our many experiences dealing with our own BS and other people's. We also literally have less energy to tolerate the drama that comes with having bad boundaries. But fear not, you don't have to wait until you're walking around holding your sore hip all day to get good at setting awesome boundaries. You can get started right now: Become aware of what your patterns are, practice slowing yourself down in situations where you're tempted to compromise the boundaries you truly need to set, and bravely step up and claim your space. When it comes to having a boundary issue of too much no, here are some good ways to break down your walls and let the yeses flow in and out:

- **Take stock of your needs.** If you're a person with a too-much-no boundary issue, you most likely have trouble recognizing that you have needs at all. In order to unearth some specifics and discover some places where you may need to let down your walls, think of a habit you'd like to form and do this exercise in the context of whatever habit you choose. For example, let's say you're going to get into the habit of playing tennis five times a week. You're obviously going to have to put yourself out there and find other people to play with, and you're going to have to put yourself and all your bad shots on display on the court for all to see. If you want to improve your backhand, you'll need to ask a pro for lessons or perhaps approach someone on a nearby court who's clearly got an amazing swing and ask them for tips. You'll have to say yes to showing up to play on the days when you don't feel like it, in order not to let your partners down. You'll need to carve out time to play and might need to ask a friend to pick your kids up at school or ask your partner to meet the plumber at the house because you've got a game scheduled.

- **Deal with your fear.** Here are some fears that might pop up around saying yes in the scenario above: If you ask people to play tennis with you, they may say no and you'll feel rejected. They may say yes and you may discover, after playing with them a few times, that they can't hit a ball over a net to save their lives or that they're intolerable windbags and now you feel trapped. Or they may discover that you're not very good or that they don't like you very much and you'll feel rejected. You may look stupid in front of other people when you hit a bad shot, you may lose your temper, and you may trip on the net in a mid-victory leap and never live it down. You may feel needy and annoying by asking your friend and your partner to help you out, and you may discover you think tennis is for the birds and be irritated that you've wasted your time and money on checking it out.

Once you've got your list of fears, notice any that really hit home for you. For example, let's break down the fear that your new tennis partners discover that you're not very good and that they don't really like you. What if this is true? *Then we'll probably have an awkward conversation where they tell me it's not working out or I'll make an excuse to quit.* Then what? *Then I'll feel stupid and embarrassed.* Then what? *Then I guess I'll have to find other people to play with.* Uncomfortable? Yes. The end of the world? No. Yet this discomfort has, so far, kept you caught in the pattern of no, so this next exercise about owning your yeses is really important.

- **Own your yeses.** Saying no all the time has a lot to do with protecting your ego, being terrified of criticism, rejection or being smothered, and fearing loss of control and love. The more you can identify as someone who doesn't take things personally, the easier it will be to let down your guard. See yourself as someone who laughs off being rejected or saddled with the task of having to inform an annoying tennis partner you've found someone else who's a better fit. Lighten up. Realize that saying yes is how you get in on life, and that life is much more enjoyable when lived fully. Envision the word "yes" as light, fluffy, and bright, and the word "no" as dark, solitary, and heavy. Be grateful for all the ease and help and love and fun that yes will bring into your life and start cracking yourself open.

- **Know who trips you up the most.** Which people do you have the hardest time opening up to and why? Get clear on the specifics, break down any fears that come up, and take baby steps putting yourself out there. For example, if you have a friend who's always looked up to you and you're scared to be vulnerable or weak in front of them because you don't want to disappoint them, start by sharing a small fear you have or a small problem and ask for their help. If there's someone you love who you fear will smother you with their neediness if you let them in at all, slowly open the gates, but only a crack at a time. For example, tell them you only have ten minutes to chat but would love to hear about their latest breakup. Identify the people you're interested in moving closer to and come up with specific things you can ask of them or things you can do for them, and tiptoe your way into being more intimate.

- **Practice in a safe space.** Ask a stranger to hold the door open for you, or get into the habit of opening the door for others. Give an unexpected compliment to a good friend or do an unasked-for favor for your partner and notice how great it feels. Do as many little yes-type things as you can think of to rewire your brain and make it understand that yes means good.

- **Learn the language of yes.** Learning the language of yes means really getting to know and recognize those moments when you will best be served by cracking open the protective shell around your heart and sharing. Learn to ask for help, advice, affection, and whatever else you need, and let others know you're there for them in return. Slow down, tune in, and be a great listener and a brave sharer of your own feelings. If you're going to learn how to say yes, you're going to have to embrace a little bit of cringe-y discomfort:

- **Remember that while you're the star of your own life, you're a supporting cast member at best in other people's lives.** Cry in front of the vet when they take Boots Rodriguez, your toothless old cat, into the back for a biopsy instead of swallowing your tidal wave of tears. They've seen people cry before; it's no big deal.

- **Speak your mind, articulate your needs.** Tell someone you love them when you're feeling verklempt. Admit you're scared, lonely, or could use a pal to look over your online dating profile even though you're mortified about posting it in the first place. As much as you don't think you need to, learning to let the love in and let your love out will help you to free up everything that seems rigid or stuck in your life.

- **Accept that communicating well is work.** You're allowed to admit that it's hard for you to open up, so cut yourself some slack and trust that anyone who's worth being more intimate with will cut you some slack too.

3. **Too controlly + the things/people/situations you want to control or that want to control you = a whole slew of murkiness, isolation, resentment, and bad behavior.**

My sister, Jill, is five years younger than I am, and as in many big sister/little sister relationships, she looked up to me and I spent much of my time rolling my eyes and trying to shake her off my leg. Until I got hungry, that is. We used to play a "game" where I'd tell her: *Run downstairs, make me and my friend peanut butter and jelly sandwiches, and grab us a couple of glasses of milk while you're at it, and I'll time you. Let's see if you can beat your record of, um, six minutes and twenty-seven seconds!* Jill would tear off to the kitchen while my friend and I resumed playing dolls who work at a dentist's office, only to be interrupted by Jill and our lunch many minutes later. I, of course, didn't bother to keep track of her time, and made some random guess when presented with her eager, expectant (and, in guilt-ridden hindsight, very cute) face. *Oh yeah, six minutes and forty-seven seconds. You came so close! I know you can beat it next time. Now get out of my room.*

Controllers come in many forms. Some controllers manipulate people into doing stuff for them that they wouldn't normally do by making it seem fun; some are expert guilt-trippers or seducers; some excel at wearing people down until they give them what they want; and some are full-on bullies. Controllers generally don't give a hoot about other people's boundaries and have lots of trouble hearing the word "no," as in, they don't really hear it at all.

Another fun form of exerting control is by inserting yourself inappropriately into the lives of others by constantly offering unsolicited advice, spending more time on bettering their lives than you do on bettering your own, and/or fully interloping your way into someone else's business: *I'm going to take care of my newly divorced best friend and her children, move in with them and cook for them, become indispensable, and then get super angry and resentful when she finds a new man and moves on.*

Take a moment to think about any ways in which you have not-so-great boundaries around control. Pay attention to the sneaky ways that control can mask itself as simply being helpful, as looking out for someone, or as being a good friend. Investigate the roles you play in other people's lives and start questioning your motives: Are you truly trying to help them? Are you inserting yourself to feel needed? Are you kinda obsessed? Listen to your intuition, and if it's telling you that someone in your life has gotten a little too close for comfort, trust that feeling. Start taking a deeper look at your actions and motives around control, and take a moment to notice how the actions of the people around you make you feel as we run through the exercise again. Because boundary issues around control are a bit different from the previous two we've worked through, I'm going to tweak the exercise slightly:

- **Know who trips you up the most.** Get mighty honest with yourself and think about the people in your life whom you try to control or whose lives are most gooily enmeshed with yours. Is there a friend whom you check in with every day, maybe even several times a day, whom you use as a platonic substitute for an intimate relationship? Is there anyone whom you constantly heap unsolicited advice onto and whom you spend an inordinate amount of time thinking about how to "fix"? Do you make your assistant do things like vacuum your office, answer snotty texts from your ex that you don't want to deal with, or other tasks outside their job description? Do you smother your kid with your emotional needs, making him or her, instead of a friend, spouse, or shrink, a sounding board for your loneliness, fears, marital problems, and regrets that you didn't experiment more in college?

- **Take stock of your needs.** What need are you attempting to meet by trying to fix other people's problems? Does it make you feel valuable, smart, seen, loved, or powerful? Are you focused on saving your friend's marriage because you can't face focusing on all the problems with yours? Does manipulating your neighbor into mowing your lawn after he's done mowing his make you feel connected to him and less isolated? What hole is your need to control attempting to fill?

- **Deal with your fear.** What fears came up when you imagined letting go of the needs you listed above? For example, let's say you backed off from being so involved in your friend's troubled marriage. You're still there for her, but you're no longer available to pick apart every text her husband sends her, you don't listen to her cavalcade of complaints night after night over a bottle of rosé, and you don't spend your free time researching hilarious cartoons about how stupid men are to send to her. Instead, you set a boundary and tell her you'll discuss solutions with her but you'll no longer wallow in the complaining. Taking the focus off her opens up new space for you to face your own life. What fears come up with that? Perhaps you've been putting off telling your spouse you want to quit your lucrative job as an attorney to become a full-time glass blower and that you need them to pick up the tab for a while? Or maybe you're scared to admit that your marriage is joyless and that you need to end it, or maybe you've got fears around not being valuable and needed and "in control" of someone else's life? Get clear on your fears, go through the process of breaking them down, and expose them as the little pipsqueaks they really are.

- **Own your surrender.** Imagine yourself leaning back and watching the person you hover over most doing their thing without your input. Envision yourself as a relaxed, helpful, loved, valued person who happily helps when needed and who lets others learn lessons they need to learn on their own. See yourself as a separate, whole, complete, loving person who is able to create whatever you desire in your own life.

- **Learn the language of surrender.** Recognizing and communicating from a place of surrender is all about coming from a place of trust instead of fear. Practice interrupting your impulse to fix, placate, call out, soapbox, push back against, or even agree with something. Take a breath, slow down, and keep these things in mind as you learn to ease into the surrender state:

  - **The language of surrender is sometimes silence.** Practice just listening instead of offering advice and suggestions. Get good at saying phrases like *Do you need some help? How can*

I best support you? Do you want ideas or are you just looking for someone to listen? Thanks for your offer to help but I think this is something I need to do on my own, and *I'm happy to help with X but I can't help with Y.*

- **Learn to speak with and listen to more than just voices.** Pay attention to the body language and the, um, verbal language of someone saying *Back off, no thanks, mind yer own fucking business,* and then do as asked.

The better you get at setting healthy boundaries of your own and respecting the boundaries of others, the more easy, successful, and joyful your life and everyone else's will be. As we embark on creating this new habit of yours, being able to identify, whip out, and masterfully set into place whatever boundary you require will help you cultivate the staying power that may have eluded you in your habit attempts in the past. Badass boundaries are every habit superhero's secret weapon.

QUIT BEING ENERGETICALLY TRIGGERED BY OTHERS, JIM, 45

I have to deal with an intense, aggressive person on a regular basis and he triggers the hell out of me. I really wanted to get some control over myself, to not take the bait and to not get all worked up, so I decided to make a habit out of staying aware and remembering to take a beat when I feel this guy launching. I think to myself, *This person is getting squirrelly. . . . Let him, but don't participate in that squirrel factor.* It's easy when his intensity isn't directed at me, because it doesn't feel like an attack and therefore I don't have the "fight-or-flight" response. When it does become personal, which it has, I have to really work hard at finding inner calm and resetting my reaction—very hard to do, as my inclination is to top his intensity with my own. But the awareness of that involuntary response of wanting to fight back is what actually stops me from doing so. That's my trigger.

Use the negative urge to react as a positive trigger: When you feel yourself getting worked up, use it as a reminder to pause, take a breath, and make a better choice.

The trigger reminds me that I'm in control of my responses and to be thoughtful about them. I feel myself getting jittery, my hands get very cold, and my body gets tight, all at the same time. And that physical discomfort causes me to have a quick internal monologue. I remind myself to calm down, to slow my breathing to counter the adrenaline rush. I recognize the feeling I'm having and let myself disapprove of how that person is making me feel, but I don't get entangled by the way I feel. Then I think about how the next words out of my face are going to have an effect, and what do I want that effect to ultimately be, which is to make me feel well and whole, but also to be heard and respected.

After the interaction is over, I feel solid and empowered, whereas in the past I would be all jacked up and upset for hours. I don't feel like this is passivity or acquiescence, but rather strength, because I'm being self-aware and making evolved, difficult, positive choices in the picosecond that this is all happening.

CHAPTER 3

SHAPESHIFTING INTO THE NEW YOU

A friend of mine recently called my attention to a habit I didn't even know I had. Apparently, after I drink something particularly satisfying, I follow it up with a lip smack and an *ahhhh!* I'm sure that my audible celebration of a sip well taken started out as a joke, but because I did it so often, my dramatic drinking became a habit that, to my amuzehorror, I now realize I do *even when I'm alone.*

> What you make fun of most,
> you become. Mock wisely.

We are all riddled with habits—habits we're aware of and habits we're oblivious to, habits we love, habits we hate, habits we love/hate, and habits that just kind of are what they are: *Here I go, putting on underpants again.* I don't think very many of us spend a whole lot of time thinking about the habits we do or don't have, but as you prepare to create a new habit, taking stock of what you've already got going on is beneficial because:

- It's inspiring to realize how many excellent habits you have.

- Becoming aware of your not-so-great habits enables you to change them.

- It's always nice to take the time to get to know yourself better.

- You can pick up useful tricks and identify avoidable obstacles by studying your existing habits, which will come in handy as you create future ones.

In order to familiarize yourself with your habits, please get your notebook and make three lists: five good habits that you seem to have always had (behaviors that you don't consciously remember creating but that are very much a part of your identity), five habits that you've intentionally

and successfully created and/or quit, and five habit upgrades that you'd love to make.

At first you may have trouble coming up with stuff for
your lists, but stick with it and I promise you, the longer
you sit there and think, the more ideas will pop into your
head. For example, here's what I came up with for myself:

- **Five good habits that I've always had:** Being tidy,
  being quick and consistent with my pleases and
  thank-yous, encouraging others, being grateful,
  stopping to smell all flowers in my path.

- **Five intentionally created or ditched habits:** Quitting smoking, hydrating every morning upon waking, making daily check-ins on Mom, letting stress
  go more quickly, being more emotionally in tune/
  available.

- **Five habit upgrades I'd love to make:** Slow down,
  become a more active activist, quit complaining,
  don't groan whenever I get out of a chair (another
  one that started as a joke and that I now perform in
  public, loudly), sing more.

Research shows that in order for us to really stick to a
habit, we have to believe in our ability to change. If you
don't yet have evidence that you can transform whatever

habit it is that you're working on, even if you have *proof* that you've tried to change and failed in the past, you have to believe that you can do it anyway—or else you will seriously half-ass creating this new habit, if you ass it at all.

Look at the first two lists you just made, the good habits you just naturally seem to have and the habits you've been intentional about, and take a moment to get a little stuck up about how inspiring and capable you are. You chose to make these habits part of your identity, whether you realized you were doing it or not, which means you can choose to welcome in the habits you've got on your third list, the habit upgrades you'd love to make.

Believing that you're capable of doing something is easiest when you've got proof. But if you're attempting something you've either never tried before or have tried and failed to do, believing it's possible can be achieved at first simply by making the decision to believe. Just believing isn't as hard to accomplish as you might think. We humans decide to believe stuff all the time, with little or no proof that it's possible or real: We decide to believe in a god; we decided to believe we can go to the Moon; we decide to believe that our new boyfriend is not distant, unavailable, and uninterested in us because he's got really nice arms and a boat. Belief is a muscle, and when you're changing a stubborn old bad habit and really stretching yourself, a hell-bent decision is the perfect personal trainer to get your belief in shape.

For example, when I became unavailable to be broke anymore, I had a teeny, tiny inkling of belief that I could be financially successful someday, but my conviction was so wimpy and shaky that I needed to build a fortress of determined decidedness around it to keep my belief from withering and dying. In the early days, I decided to keep pushing myself to do all the stuff I had to do that scared the hell out of me—get over my fraud complex and announce to the world that I was a coach, put up a website with a picture of myself wearing makeup on it, charge actual money for my services—and to keep looking for proof that what I desired was possible. This decision slowly but surely strengthened my belief that I, Jen Sincero, would one day pay extra to check a bag instead of wearing all my sweaters onto the plane and doing carry-on for free. I didn't get started on my journey fully believing I could make money; at first I decided just to believe I could.

> Commit to change and
> conviction will follow.

Once you identify a habit that you'd like to work on for the remainder of this book, I'll show you how to use your almighty power of decision to help anchor it in. Refer now to the third list you made—the five habit upgrades you'd love to make—and either pick a habit off this list or choose something else that has real meaning for you. Ideally you'll choose something that inspires you, but not something that's so gigantic you give up before you make it through the work we're about to do: *I'm going to jog ten miles every morning starting tomorrow even though I ran through the airport the other day and had to call for a wheelchair halfway to my gate. I ran track in college, though, so I got this.* The purpose here is to give yourself the chance to fully experience the habit-forming process and to see some real results—not to get frustrated, quit, or pull a muscle your first day out.

Please pick one and only one habit that you're either eager to cultivate or that you can't wait to drag to the curb, something that would give you:

- a sense of being the person you know you're meant to be;

- a sense of empowerment;

- an improved quality of life;

- a sense of accomplishment (meaning this new habit feels attainable but still large and important and bragworthy).

Before you get too attached to the habit itself, think about the desire driving you to choose this habit, and do your best to make sure you've made the wisest choice possible. For example, if your desire is to lose thirty pounds but you hate dieting and have never stuck with any particular diet for more than a few weeks, maybe, instead of focusing on losing weight and depriving yourself of your favorite foods, you need to focus on developing the habit of eating what you like, but just eating less of it. If your desire is to have a better relationship with your partner, maybe achieving that isn't about getting into the habit of going on date nights and cooking more dinners together, but about really listening to them or telling them how much you appreciate them or noticing and being grateful for all the reasons you chose to be with them in the first place. I'm in the habit of having wine whenever I eat red sauce or a steak, but I'm also in the habit of being a total pantywaist when it comes to drinking these days—I can't sleep and I get hungover from just one glass. I toyed with quitting drinking altogether, but that seemed rather over-dramatic considering I hardly drink at all, so now I have a tiny little sake cup that I sip my wine out of (smack, *ahhhhh!*), and this little thimbleful allows me to enjoy some wine without being in pain the next morning. I met my desire not to feel awful by cutting back (easier habit), not by cutting myself off completely (more difficult habit), and it's done the trick. Take a moment to think about the most successful way you can design this habit to reflect your desires instead of just leaping in cold turkey, repeating past attempts that didn't work, or thoughtlessly doing what everyone else does or tells you to do.

Once you've figured out what your habit is, lock into the decision to make it happen by imagining all the details of how achieving this habit will feel. Connect with the emotions that your desire to be this new person calls up. Make this journey you're on much bigger than the new habit itself (because it is). Step fully into the identity of the person you'll be when you embody this habit and fall in love with who you're becoming. Realize that becoming the kind of person who does what you're setting out to do is an act of self-love and respect, that forming this habit means you believe in yourself, and that you're doing what it takes to give your awesome self everything you desire and deserve.

> Focus your attention on the desires fueling the habit, not on the habit itself.

Deciding to change your life means you've made a tacit agreement with yourself that you're capable of and deserve this new identity. Deciding to upgrade your life is basically being super nice to yourself; it's like saying, *Self, you matter, and I'm gonna roll out the red carpet for you.* Sitting around doing nothing, ignoring your health and happiness, and pretending you don't have the discipline to change the things you'd love to change are also decisions, decisions that mean you've made an agreement with yourself that you're incapable of, uninterested in, or perhaps underserving of this new habit. I know, right? Why would you be that way to your sweet self? I'm assuming that since you've picked up this book, you're already on board with the red carpet version, but lord knows we can all get wobbly in our resolve, so we need to stay aware of, and work with, our whole selves, not just the parts we proudly parade around for all to see.

Being aware of both of these possible identities—the you that's in love with yourself and the you that's not feeling so special—will help you stick to your decision to stay the course, which is why I want you to now write down the details of what both of these identities look like, and especially what they feel like. Write a day-in-the-life scenario for both versions, from getting out of bed (or off the futon), making your coffee, getting dressed: What stresses are running through your mind as the sad-sack you? What are you excited about as you move through your day as the upgraded you? Paint a real, detailed picture of each version of your life to remind yourself that they're both totally available to you depending on what you choose to decide. Use the fear and loathing of the not-so-great version to propel you out and away from it, and the thrill and anticipation of the awesome one to lift you upward and toward it. You will eventually cut ties completely with the old, less-motivated you—you honestly eventually won't even remember what it feels like to be that person once you've fully owned your new identity—but fear of staying stuck in old bad habits can be a helpful tool in the beginning to get you off your butt and do what needs to be done.

For example, when I decided to quit smoking, I no longer wanted to have a disgusting cough and reek of smoke, but even more importantly, I wanted to be the kind of person who respected my health, who showed my dear body that I loved it, my body that, with pretty much zero help from me, managed to still work and take me all over the world and provide me with incredible pleasure in so many ways. I wanted to stop being that person who had to walk out of movies early because my nicotine craving was tugging on my sleeve. I wanted to be in control of my life, not controlled by some dumb drug. Now that I haven't smoked in decades, I barely remember how awful it felt to be tethered to that old habit, but those icky feelings were very helpful motivators on my journey to quitting. Good habits are about who you decide to be, not what you decide to do, so get mighty clear and worked up over the image of yourself succeeding, and mighty uninterested and grossed out by the image of yourself staying stuck, and use these feelings and emotions to help you stay on course.

We are creatures who are driven by the often opposing forces of emotion and logic, and if it came down to a wrestling match, my money would definitely be on emotions for the win. I mean, think about it—how many times have you done something that you know in your sensible, grown-up mind is a really bad idea, but in your heart it sounds insanely fun or thrilling or irresistible: *OMG, they're having an adoption fair? I know we haven't ever discussed getting a dog but we have to adopt this puppy even though we're so busy and our hands are already full with two kids under the age of three because . . . look at that nose. And we definitely need to get his sister while we're at it so he has a pal.*

You need the double whammy of getting both your heart and your head on board with your decision in order to lock in this new habit. We tend to give much more airtime to our logical sides, so I really want you to make the effort not only to feel into the details of your emotions but to revisit them as often as possible.

> Your heart, not your head, is the keeper of the flame beneath your fanny.

You know who quits eating French fries no problem? The guy whose doctor tells him he'll be looking down the barrel of the great beyond in two months if he doesn't knock it off right now. The goal here is to conjure up a similar dedication, one full of heart, head, and *Holy shit, I'm on it*, without necessarily involving such a pressing, mortal ultimatum.

Decide to embody the identity that represents the desires in your heart. Decide to take risks, to fail, to look ridiculous, to be victorious, to be as true to yourself as you can possibly be. Decide to love yourself through all the trials and errors and false starts. Stay focused on your brave decision to change your life rather than focusing on any expectations of perfection or any desires to succeed right out of the gate. Get clear on what will happen if you decide to pretend you can't hear your heart; lay out the specifics. What are the consequences? Who will you be stuck being if you tell yourself that you can't have what you want or that going after your desires isn't worth the effort? How do you want to ride out your one and only wild trip through the bananas journey called life as the you who is you?

I want to stress here that this habit-forming, ass-kicking stuff is all about what you desire, not what you think you should desire or what anyone else tells you you should do. We're all different creatures, and one person's version of success may be sitting around looking at birds all day with their fellow ornithological-type pals while another person's version might be helping feed the hungry children of the world. Your life, your choice. I also want to stress that not everyone has a quest that they absolutely know is the very thing they've been put here to do. You may just be looking to feel a certain way or to explore and discover what it is that turns you on. There is no right or wrong; there's just tuning in to the compass that is your heart and heading in the direction that it's pointing you.

Here are a few last thoughts for the road to keep in mind as we head into new-habit land:

1. Stick to this one habit for the entire 21-day program. Do not pretend the reason your habit is getting challenging or boring or me no wanna is because you picked something that isn't right for you. Don't convince yourself that you chose to make doing a hundred sit-ups a day your habit when what you really should have chosen to do is make a gratitude list every night. Anything worth upgrading in your life is going to be challenging, or else you would've already upgraded it. The ever-popular bait and switch is such an easy out and such a great way to make no progress ever, because there will always be an unlimited supply of "better," more novel, and not-yet-boring ideas that you can hop back and forth among for the rest of your life. Do not stray and thou shalt be victorious.

2. Get back on the horse immediately if you happen to fall off. If you're quitting smoking but got a little boozy the other night and took a drag off a cigarette, or if you ate a meatball at your friend's wedding even though you're going vegan, forget about it and start again right here, right now. The key to succeeding in spite of slipups is jumping back in right away instead of wallowing

(luxuriating?) in your failure and bemoaning the fact that you're not perfect.

> Perfectionism is just procrastination in a fancy outfit.

If you hit pause on your new habit routine for more than a day or two after a slipup, your old ways will come back so fast you won't even remember that you were trying to change in the first place. Your old, bad habits have the home-field advantage. They've been with you much longer (your entire life?) than has this fabulous new habit you're nurturing, so they have a much stronger support system, what with muscle memory, familiarity, and your old identity all rooting for them. If you give them an inch they will take a mile, so a speedy recovery is epically important if you drop the ball.

Every moment of every day you have the chance to start over with a clean slate. Success is all about forgiving, forgetting, tenacity, and getting your ass back on track prontissimo.

3. If you've tried to adopt or ditch this habit before, think about what you can do differently this time. And more importantly, what you can do differently *that is wildly outside your comfort zone*. For example, if you've tried in the past to start a regular practice of swimming laps every morning and have stuck with it for a few months only to eventually peter out, hire a swim coach who shows up a couple of times a week and whom you (a) pay a lot, (b) set goals with, or (c) are scared of. When you travel, research hotels that have pools or pools nearby so you can keep your habit rolling. Sign up and train for a race and tell all your friends about it. Go to therapy to explore any psychological blocks you may have around successfully achieving your goal.

If you want to make this habit stick this time, do it differently this time. Become the person who isn't screwing around, really identify as the person who's already nailed this habit, and see yourself and your swimming habit through their eyes.

> When you change who you're being, you begin seeing everything through new eyes: You suddenly notice awesome parts of yourself that you never gave much credit to, and you realize that you're one mighty motherfucker.

It's like waking up and suddenly grasping what your pals have been ribbing you about for years—you're totally in love with your best friend. Nothing about your friend has changed; you were just looking at them through the eyes of your old self, who could only see them as your buddy.

4. As you move through the day-by-day process, pay attention to which suggestions work best for you and write them down in your notebook so you can use them again and again.

Work through the 21 days as often as you need to until your habit's on autopilot and you no longer need the training wheels provided by this book. For example, once you finish your first round and get to Day 21, if you still feel a bit shaky, start over from Day 1 and take it day by day if that feels appropriate. Or, if you feel like there were standout days in the course that really helped you and you don't need to do every single day again, repeat just those days until your new habit is lodged in your noggin. It's up to you; you know what works best for you.

How long it will take to cultivate your new habit is up for grabs—I've read studies that say anchoring a habit takes twenty-one days, I've also heard fourteen days, and I've also heard it takes sixty repetitions. But in my experience, from what I've seen, each new habit takes as long as that individual habit takes. For example, after fifty-four years of half-assing it, I developed the habit of flossing my teeth religiously every single morning in about fourteen seconds after my new dental hygienist came at me wearing a face mask and those alarming, see-right-through-to-your-soul dentist binoculars. She placed various sharp and pointy tools on a tray while showing me photo after photo of the diseased and decaying gums of those foolish enough not to heed her dental credo of "floss or fester." Before that moment I was strictly a post-corn-on-the-cob-type flosser, or I'd toothpick out whatever got lodged in there after gnawing something off a bone; maybe I'd share the wealth and hit the rest of my teeth while I was at it, maybe I wouldn't. Now I flip over tables and chairs and push slow-moving seniors out of my way in a rush to get home if I realize I forgot to floss.

I suggest we all head into this journey of self-transformation with focus, excitement, compassion, and determination, and that we remember to remain very impressed with ourselves for showing up day after day and doing what it takes to make the world a better place. And, of course:

> Trust that the Universe always delivers right on time.

STOPPED BITING HER NAILS, DIANA, 41

I started biting my nails at around seven years old when my parents got divorced, so it really took some psychological work to stop doing it, since it was pretty deeply buried and related to that trauma. One of the things that really helped me stop was going to therapy as an adult. I learned to manage depression and anxiety in general, and also how to stop taking it out on my nails.

Along with going to therapy I started journaling, stream of consciousness, every day, first thing in the morning. Writing helps me with all my habits because it keeps me connected to my emotions and to my psychological self and helps me get all that inner stuff out onto the page, so I don't have to act it out in these unhealthy and unconscious ways.

In addition to the emotional stuff that was going on, I also had to address the physical part of biting my nails, and that work needed to be very conscious too. I decided to start getting manicures every week, and that became almost religious, like my journaling. I crowded out my gross old habit of biting my nails with my new habit of getting manicures.

Crowd out an old bad habit by creating a new behavior that doesn't allow the old behavior to coexist.

Not only did the manicures get rid of the raggedy edges that invited me to bite them off, but they made me think, *Hey, there's polish on my nails, I don't want to eat polish. Who knows what's in that stuff?* Plus they looked so pretty, I didn't want to mess them up. Then I started being happy with the way they looked, which was a whole different relationship with my hands. My hands were always painful, bloody messes and now they looked great and didn't hurt anymore. I guess I also crowded out the habit of having picked at, hurting hands with being in the habit of having beautiful, healthy ones. Anyway, that was all decades ago and I haven't bitten a nail since.

CHAPTER 4

21 DAYS TO BADASS HABITS

Now that we've gotten your mind primed and your habit picked out, we're going to get down to bizniss. This section of the book is designed to be used as a course that you move through one day at a time for 21 days. By slowing your roll and taking it day by day, you'll prevent yourself from going into overwhelm, you'll stay engaged, and you'll give your new habit time to sink in. Think of this course as your accountability partner who shows up every morning with a helpful tool, a new insight, an impressed raised eyebrow, a hug of encouragement, and/or a loving kick in the rear.

Write down the habit you're going to work on in your

notebook. In all caps. This habit you've chosen is going to become your obsession, your teacher, your muse for self-actualization. You will focus on this habit and do everything you can to embody it, and then once you do, it'll just be a regular part of who you are, it'll become nothing special, you'll probably stop picking it up at the airport and sending it flowers because you'll be so accustomed to having it around you'll barely even notice it's there. And then, because we're all creatures in a constant state of transformation, you'll shift your attention onto some newer, fresher, even more compelling habit, and you'll have the confidence, know-how, and tools to make it yours as well.

Alrighty, let's do this!

DAY 1: YOUR MANTRA OF MIGHTINESS

I am pleased to report that one of the most powerful tools for habit transformation is also one of the simplest—the almighty mantra. You already use mantras all the time whether you realize it or not: *I can't lose this pregnancy weight, I have excellent parking karma, I hate my ears, Life is good, I always date crazy people.* You have already created the "reality" in which you exist via the thoughts, beliefs, mantras, habits, and actions you've repeated over and over throughout your life.

> You will experience whatever you believe. And you will believe whatever you repeatedly tell yourself is true.

Which is why ditching crummy mantras and consciously creating and endlessly repeating mantras that are aligned with what you'd like to experience and who you'd like to become is a powerful way to change your life.

Our brains are just like eager dogs who want to please us. They'll lap up whatever information we feed them, jump in the car and join us on whatever road we're headed down, no matter how bonkers our itinerary may be, and match whatever energy we put out: *I have no idea what's going on but the humans are dancing around and laughing so I'm gonna bark and run in circles and maybe even pee a tiny bit about it.*

Training your brain is like training a dog to sit or come or go lie down. It's all about meaning, simplicity, treats, and repetition. For example, when I was in the habit of being broke and finally committed to dumping my old "truth" of *I can't afford it,* I began using the new mantra *Money flows to me easily and freely.* This new mantra worked so well because the words struck an emotional chord with me, I understood that money truly did flow easily to some people, and although I didn't yet know how it would flow to me, I was excited by the possibility and energized by the challenge to stretch myself and make it happen. This mantra also trained my focus to sniff out any crumbs of truth I could find that made me feel hopeful and kept me looking for more and bigger crumbs, and because of all this, I felt inspired to say it a million times a day until it stuck.

I also want to mention that *Money flows to me easily and freely* sounded insanely lofty and corny to me at first, but it worked like a charm because it challenged my specific issues around money. (I'm going to break down how it did in a second.) As we embark on designing the perfect mantra for you, I want you not to focus on any eye-rolls or as-ifs that the words may conjure up but rather on the emotions they cause you to feel and how masterfully they nail your negative talk to the wall. No matter how far-fetched and stupid your mantra may sound today, you will give nary two craps about that when you're luxuriating in the reality it describes down the road. Trust me, there ain't nothing corny or lofty about money flowing to me easily and freely now that it does these days.

To come up with a mantra for the habit you're about to create, it's helpful to look at opposing mantras and the unhelpful beliefs you're currently, and very often unconsciously, lugging around in regard to this habit. So grab your notebook and let's clean out the crazy corners of your mind.

Sit quietly and imagine yourself embodying your new habit. Bring up as many details as you can, and really feel what it's like to be this new and improved version of yourself. What specific aspects of your day-to-day life have changed as a result of who you've become? How does your body feel? What gets you pumped up? What are you able to do as this new person that you weren't able to do before? How do you describe yourself? How do you look? How does this new habit positively affect the people in your life? What else has shifted in your life as a result of this habit? While you absorb all the specifics of embodying this habit, be on the lookout for the excuses and objections that rear their heads and write them down the second they appear.

To use my former financially challenged self as an example, when I decided I was going to get serious about making money, I sat and imagined what it would feel like to have a consistent stream of two-thousand- and five-thousand-dollar checks arriving in the mail every week. I imagined driving the Audi I wanted to buy. I visualized paying off my credit-card debt. I saw myself leaving huge tips, donating money, surprising my friends and family with flowers, plane tickets, and ponies, and I luxuriated in the relief of finally being financially free.

At first, imagining this future felt thrilling, but as I sat there leaning into the specifics of what having money meant to me, other voices began bubbling up from my subconscious swamp: *There's no way I could ever make that kind of money. Where the hell would it come from? The Unicorn Bank? I can't afford to get that car, plus it's going to cost a fortune to fix and it takes premium gas—hello?! I'm not the kind of person who makes money. And even if by some miracle I did make money, everyone who knows me would think I sold out. My friends would make fun of me, resent me, or suddenly act like I'm too good for them and dump me. I'd have to do stuff I hate to make money, it would be really hard, and I don't trust that it would stick around anyway. I'm going to be sleeping on a futon for the rest of my life.*

I wrote several pages' worth of negative spewage about my nonability to make money, how gross I felt about money, and how losery I felt about myself, and I must admit, it was pretty damn sobering and sad. I was already aware of how helpless and frustrated and unsuccessful I felt, but lordy lord, to sit and stare at the mental toxins I'd been unconsciously pouring all over myself and my world—it was quite the wake-up call.

> Taking the time to write stream of consciousness about an area in your life where you're feeling stuck is one of the best ways to smoke out the sneaky, sucky, hidden beliefs that are holding you back.

I took my many pages of pathos, read through them again, and highlighted the gnarliest beliefs that triggered the deepest, most upsetting reactions from me. Then, in order to write my mantra, I followed five basic rules:

1. Take three to five of the most loaded/heartbreaking specifics of all your objections and write those down. (It can be a bit *Sophie's Choice*, so follow your emotions—really feel into everything you've written and notice which things piss you off/make you cry/confound you the most.)

2. Write the opposite of these negative beliefs, using words and phrases that have meaning and emotion.

3. Start brainstorming new mantras, keeping your words positive (it's not *I feel so good not smoking* but rather *I love my pink, healthy lungs*). Make every word count. Make every word loaded with the feels.

4. Keep your writing in the present tense.

5. Keep your mantra short.

For example, here are the specific beliefs and objections that triggered me the most when I read over the pages I wrote about my relationship with money:

1. *Making money isn't in the cards for me; it's never going to happen.*

2. *It's always going to be hard/fun-free for me to make money.*

3. *If I do somehow miraculously make money, it will be a fluke and the stream will eventually dry up.*

4. *It's not safe for me to make money; I'll lose friends and family and be heartbroken.*

Once I had my short list of most meaningful/hurtful beliefs, I started flipping them around to write my new mantra:

1. *Making money isn't in the cards for me; it's never going to happen* became *I am surrounded by money, it's all over the place, and it flows to me effortlessly and joyfully.*

2. *It's always going to be hard/fun-free for me to make money* became *Money is easy and fun to make, I love making money, and I'm great at making money.*

3. *If I do somehow miraculously make money, it will be a fluke and the stream will eventually dry up* became *Money is my pal, it's meant for me, it's here for me, and it flows to me consistently.*

4. *It's not safe for me to make money; I'll lose friends and family and be heartbroken* became *I can have both*

money and love; my friends and family will be happy for
me; money and love are meant for me.

Then I extracted all the new, positive sayings and edited them down, taking out words that felt repetitive and/or not as charged as others, and added new words that had more juice. (Hang in there; this is important and we're almost done.) My new list looked like this:

1. *I am surrounded by money and it flows to me easily.*

2. *Money is easy and fun to make. I love making money.*

3. *Money is meant for me.*

4. *I can have both money and love. I am free to make money.*

Now, we could all have mantras that are several paragraphs long if we're going to fully address all the issues we've got around the stuff that really trips us up (right? I'm not the only one?), but we want a mantra that's tiny yet mighty so it's easy to both repeat and remember. In order to keep whittling my mantra down, when I got to this stage I felt into it and realized that ease and freedom were the concepts that really hit home for me—and that were alluded to in every positive statement I'd crafted. I felt so constricted by not being able to afford anything; so heavy, stuck, and blocked by the belief that money wasn't available to me somehow; and so frustrated by how hard it was for me to crack the code on how to make it. I mean, complete idiots made money all the time, what the hell was my problem?

I singled out the words "money," "easy," "fun," "love," "free," and "flow" because they felt the most charged— they were light and powerful and liberating and they countered the dark, hard, heavy feelings I had. I took those words and messed around with mantras like:

- *Money is fun to make. I love it and it flows to me easily.*

- *I'm free to make money. It's easy and I'm in the flow with it.*

- *I make money freely and easily. I'm in the flow and it's fun.*

I kept moving the words around until I finally landed on something that felt both doable and insane at the same time: *Money flows to me easily and freely.* This mantra was like the foot that quickly flew into the slamming door and kept me cracked open whenever *I can't afford it* tried to sneak back and cage me in.

Write down as many versions of your mantra-in-progress as you need to, adding and switching words around until you hit on something that feels right. Don't try to address all your negative beliefs in this one mantra—the essential element here is that your mantra makes you feel energized, hopeful, inspired, and maybe a little crazy for having the audacity to believe such magnificence exists for you.

Here are some quick examples to help you create your own mantra:

New habit: Flirt with someone hot every day.

Objections: I suck at flirting; I'm scared of getting stuck talking to someone who turns out to be a drip; I'll be rejected and humiliated; I'll look desperate and stupid.

Mantra: I am sexy, open, and lovable; I attract my perfect mate with playfulness and ease.

New Habit: Quit smoking.

Objections: I've tried so many times already and failed; It's hard; I'm so addicted; I love doing it; Smoking comforts me.

Mantra: I am happy and healthy and I love being in control of my life.

New Habit: Be a better listener.

Objections: I don't even realize I'm talking so much; It's hard to catch myself; People can be so boring.

Mantra: I love to listen and learn; I'm grounded, aware, and in control of my actions.

New Habit: Take action every day to help save the rain forests.

Objections: I'm already overwhelmed; What the hell can I do that will make a difference?; I'm an ignoramus when it comes to politics; I don't know where to start or what to do.

Mantra: It's easy to make a difference; it fills me with joy and I learn as I go.

Writing your mantra is all about coming up with specific words that counter your negative beliefs and that bring up positive, meaningful, exciting emotions. This part is key—your mantra must really affect you in a deeply moving way or else you'll find yourself saying a bunch of annoying words over and over that don't inspire you to go out and make the changes you need to make.

IMPORTANT MANTRA NOTE: Don't worry if it's hard to believe your mantra at first—as long as you can feel a ping of thrill (which is your higher self doing a cartwheel), you'll know you're on the right track. Simply decide to believe it until you actually do.

Once you come up with your mantra, write it down and say it every day, all the time. Say it out loud while you're driving, in your mind waiting for takeoff, while you're walking the dog, feeding your kids, brushing your teeth, pretending to listen to someone who won't stop talking, doing the dishes, in a box with a fox. The power is all in the repetition, connecting with the feeling of excitement that the words conjure up and basking in the glory of the new reality that's hurtling toward you.

> The more you hang out in the energy of that which you desire, the more effortlessly you will attract it to you.

FINAL IMPORTANT MANTRA NOTE: If objections continue to arise as you say your new mantra, fret not, this is a good sign. The fact that your old identity is rearing up and fighting for its life means that things are shifting and that your old self feels threatened. Use your new mantra as a club to beat your objections back into their sad little holes.

DAY 2: SET YOURSELF UP

One of my favorite words in the English language is "ease." Even saying it feels good. It's like letting out a huge, relaxing exhale while slowly reclining backward as you undo your pants. You know who else loves the word "ease"? Habits. The easier you make it for them to show up, the more regularly they will. Like so many things in nature, habits follow the path of least resistance: Water is pulled by gravity around rocks, over waterfall ledges, and down streambeds in an effortless flow; birds ride air currents, updrafts, and jet streams to get where they're going with the fewest number of flaps; my movers carry my mattress through the living room, over my new white carpet, and into the bedroom instead of going around via the uncarpeted kitchen because the white-rug route takes less time.

Put some thought into structuring your new habit to make it as effortless and as easy as possible while you're at the beginning of your journey, and you'll be more likely to find yourself successful on the other end. And please, go beyond the obvious. Get creative—there are so many ways you can set yourself up physically, emotionally, spiritually, and intellectually. Sometimes the littlest things can make the most gigantic difference, so as you're brainstorming, make sure you consider no tweak too tiny.

For example, if your new habit is to get yourself to the gym at six o'clock every morning, lay out your workout clothes the night before; put your coffee maker on a timer so it's already made when you get up; prepare snacks that you can pop in your mouth when you return home; get everything ready for work so all you have to do afterward is shower, grab your stuff, and go. Do whatever you can think of, and because this time is different, because this time you're unavailable for failure, because this time you're not screwing around . . . go beyondo. Buy new workout clothes that feel special instead of schlepping off to the gym in old sweats and a ratty T-shirt, find a picture of what you want your body to look like and tape it to your alarm clock, tell a pal that each time you fail to make it to the gym you will give her three hundred dollars, find a gym as close to your house as possible, bask in the glory of your morning workout all day long, and wear a new ring that reminds you to say your mantra every time it catches your eye. Push past where you'd normally stop and find all sorts of new ways to make this habit as easy, and involve as little thought, as possible.

> Organization, scheduling, convenience, accountability to other people, constant reminders, repeating your mantra, connecting energetically with being who you're becoming, fear of looking like a moron—all of these seemingly little details will help set you up for success when creating a new habit.

Conversely, when you're quitting a bad habit, you're gonna want to create as much friction and lack of ease as possible. Eliminating bad habits from your life is all about difficulty, inconvenience, discomfort, fear, loathing, expense, repeating your mantra, connecting energetically with being who you're becoming, not wanting to look like a moron, accountability to other people, constant reminders of how much better off you are without it—the more repulsive and impossible you make this unwanted habit, the better.

Let's say you're going to quit drinking. Yes, get rid of

all the alcohol in your house; pack up and hide any champagne flutes, shakers, flasks, shot glasses, and pictures of yourself doing beer bongs in college. But also plan to meet friends at coffee shops instead of bars; tell a pal that if you slip up and take a sip, you will give her three hundred dollars each time; experiment with other fun, nonalcoholic things to drink; go to AA meetings; research all the disgusting and destructive things alcohol does to your body; and tape a picture of your cute face on your refrigerator to remind yourself how much you love and want to take care of yourself.

Get your notebook and make a list of at least fifteen things you will do to set yourself up for success. This goes for you quitters too—make a list of fifteen things you will do to make participating in your ex-habit as revolting and as big a pain in the ass as possible. And then go out and do them. Today.

Tiny tweaks add up to big changes.

. . . .

Please say your mantra right now. Say it out loud, say it to yourself, say it all day long. Feel it, see it, love it, believe it, rejoice in it, become it, repeat it, and then repeat it some more. Say it right before you fall asleep and first thing when you wake up.

. . . .

DAY 3: TRACK YOUR PROGRESS

Have you ever sat on the open tailgate of a truck, pulled your sore, throbbing feet out of their hiking boots, looked up at the mountain you just climbed, and thought, *Holy frijoles, I was just all the way up there*? Or have you ever stood at the base of a skyscraper, looked up, and marveled at the miracle towering before you that humans made with their hands and their minds?

Climbing the mountain and building the skyscraper happen step by step and floor by floor, but when you're the one hiking or the one hammering, you don't really experience much of the progress as it's happening. You're in the process of creating it, and much of the ground you gain is fairly invisible to you until you hit an overlook on the trail or finish off a substantial number of floors or stand back when you're done, point at your grand accomplishment, and regale everyone in earshot with endlessly detailed stories about how you did it.

This is much the same way our habits roll out—day by

day, plank by plank, rice cake by rice cake—until we suddenly realize one day, *Well will you look at that, I'm a size six!*

> It's much easier to stick to a habit if you feel like you're making progress, but I'm sorry to report that the majority of habit-building-and-busting routines don't offer a damn thing in the visible accomplishment department for quite some time.

But you know what is immediately satisfying? Tracking your habits (marking each day that you show up). While you may not see the actual results of the actions you take every day, you will see how many days you've stayed on course with your new habit, which is a huge accomplishment in itself.

Today I'd like you to get a calendar, an old-timey paper calendar or datebook, and dedicate it to this journey you're on. Each day that you successfully participate in your habit—eat 1,700 calories, walk three miles, say not one snarky thing to your mother, do yoga, refrain from constant apologizing, learn a new vocabulary word—

mark that day off on the calendar. Use something ceremonial to mark your calendar with, like a special pen or a gold star sticker or a heavily lipsticked kiss or perhaps, if your habit's really intense, your blood.

The simple task of acknowledging a job well done is very satisfying, and being able to look back over days and weeks and months of successfully doing what you promised yourself you'd do is even better. Tracking your habits will help you stay the course because you'll become more invested in your progress (because you can actually see it), you'll experience the fun little treat of marking it off each day, and you'll build your confidence because you now have solid proof that you're in the process of making something good happen for yourself.

Please say your mantra right now. Say it out loud, say it to yourself, say it all day long. Feel it, see it, love it, believe it, rejoice in it, become it, repeat it, and then repeat it some more. Say it right before you fall asleep and first thing when you wake up.

DAY 4: MOOCH OFF ANOTHER HABIT

make my bed religiously every morning. I can't enjoy my day if my bed's not all tight and tidy and tucked in. I even make my bed when I'm staying in a hotel, before housekeeping comes, because *what kind of animal gets up and brushes her teeth with all that twisted, wrinkled chaos just lying there staring at her?* We all have a plethora of habits built into our everyday lives, and one of the best ways to introduce a new habit is by attaching it to one that already exists. It's like carpooling: You're heading that way anyhow, might as well take another habit along for the ride.

Refer back to Chapter 3 and look at the good habits you're already participating in and see if you can barnacle a new habit, or several new habits, onto any of them. Also, write a new list of things you just happen to do every day that may not have made the original habit list (drive to work, sit down at your desk, pick up your kids, make lunch, feed the cat, put on your shoes, turn off the lights, figure out where the hell you left your phone), because these can be useful opportunities for new habits to glom on to as well.

Here are a few examples of habit sharing to help spark some ideas for you:

- While sitting on the toilet in the morning (existing habit), floss your teeth (new habit). Leave the floss by the toilet so it's right there (ease, trigger). While you're still groggy, head back to the bedroom and meditate for ten minutes (another habit added to the carpool). Set an alarm on your phone, which you've silenced, so you know when your ten-minute meditation is up (ease, organization). When you're done meditating, stretch and do a ten-minute workout (another carpool participant). Set an alarm for this too.

- If you're a coffee drinker and want to hydrate more, piggyback the drinking of water onto your existing coffee habit. Leave a giant water glass by the coffee maker (ease, trigger) so when you make your morning coffee you first fill up the water glass and down it. Make a rule that every time you have a cup of coffee, you also have a giant glass of water. You could even step it up and hydrate every time you walk by the coffee maker.

- Leave a bottle of vitamin E oil by the sink (ease). After washing your hands (existing habit), rub the oil on your beautifully unbitten fingernails (ditched habit).

- When you get behind the wheel of a car and turn it on (existing habit), pause for a moment (awareness), take a breath, and remember to stay present and calm and visualize that an older person going five miles an hour in a thirty-mile-an-hour speed zone is your frightened, confused grandpa whom you love (new habit) instead of flying into a rage-filled temper tantrum (ditched habit).

- Every time you get a text and go to read it (existing habit), say your mantra (new habit).

- While changing into your pajamas at night (existing habit), run through a gratitude list in your head (new habit).

- When you make your kids' breakfast (existing habit), visualize fitting into the beautiful dress you bought for your sister's wedding (new habit), say your mantra in your head (another new habit), and resist putting their leftover French toast into your mouth (ditched habit).

- As you walk through the door to your office at your ho-hum job (existing habit), list the reasons that you're grateful to this job (new habit), say your mantra in your head (new habit), and embody the feelings of the new, awesome career that you're in the process of creating (new habit).

• •

Please say your mantra right now. Say it out loud, say it to yourself, say it all day long. Feel it, see it, love it, believe it, rejoice in it, become it, repeat it, and then repeat it some more. Say it right before you fall asleep and first thing when you wake up.

• •

DAY 5: REFUSE TO PARTICIPATE
IN NEGOTIATIONS

don't like to play favorites but I find the concept of nonnegotiation to be one of the most powerful tools when you're adopting a new habit or breaking a nasty old one. The practice of nonnegotiation involves your mind stepping in like the stud it is, adjusting its holster, and politely ordering everyone to please move aside and clear the way while it takes full control of the situation. Here's how nonnegotiation works:

You decide that you are the kind of person who shows up everywhere on time, who is open to receiving romantic love, who is full of gratitude, who has a successful weekly podcast, who fights for the rights of others, who speaks in a curse-free, wholesome way—whatever your habit is, own it fully right now in the present moment. Now, when (not if) temptation rears its head, because you are so no-nonsense and have already identified as the person you are becoming, the things you used to enter into negotiations with do not compute anymore (*I'll just take one tiny puff; I'll blow off journaling just this morning; I'll call my congresswoman tomorrow; I'll share just this one little morsel of gossip*).

If you're dumping the habit of smoking pot, you do not negotiate about whether or not to get stoned, ever, because you are not a pot smoker, just as you wouldn't waste your time negotiating whether or not to drink a bottle of vodka for breakfast because it's not who you ARE. It's like someone making fun of you for being bald when you have a full head of hair—when you embody who you're becoming, these old negotiations seem ridiculous and unworthy of a thought, let alone a response, because they have nothing to do with who you are.

> The rapid speed with which you bypass these negotiations is paramount—use the zero-second rule.

For example, instead of reading about all the various pizza toppings they offer at a restaurant and comparing them to the salad options, pick the salad you're having and shut the menu immediately. You don't investigate pizza options because you don't eat dairy. The moment the intruder of negotiation cracks open the back door, you *choose* to stay fully embodied in who you are and kick the door shut. *I'm just gonna quickly check Facebook to see . . .* SLAM. Moving on. *I'm just gonna hit snooze and sleep . . .* SLAM. Moving on. *Ooh, is that a coconut cream pie? . . .* SLAM. Moving on. Awareness, speed, and zero tolerance are called for here.

To recap: Beware of the negotiation the moment it appears, lock into the perception of yourself as the fabulous creature that you ARE, realize this negotiation has nothing to do with you, you couldn't be less interested, in fact, you barely even noticed it because you can't relate to it at all. Move on immediately to the next thought.

• •

> Please say your mantra right now. Say it out loud, say it to yourself, say it all day long. Feel it, see it, love it, believe it, rejoice in it, become it, repeat it, and then repeat it some more. Say it right before you fall asleep and first thing when you wake up.

• •

DAY 6: ANTICIPATE YOUR EXCUSES AND DISTRACTIONS

Have you ever had a conversation like this with a friend (or, you know, yourself)?

Your friend: I can't believe Sharon told everyone I had gastric bypass surgery.

Your thought: You can't? She told your garbageman you thought he was hot after you swore her to secrecy. You said, and I quote, "I'm never telling that gasbag anything again."

Your mouth: That's awful.

Your friend: I know! It was very personal and I trusted her. I'm never telling that gasbag anything again.

Your thought: Check please!

Your mouth: Good idea.

So often when we're trying to upgrade our habits or accomplish something challenging, we fall prey to well-known, and hence easy to avoid, methods of self-sabotage and then act all, *How is it four o'clock already? Have I really spent the past two hours prepping my vegetable-garden beds when I was supposed to be memorizing my clarinet fingering chart?* Luckily, the excellent thing about being you is that you know what your dirty little secrets are. You're the expert on your A-list excuses and distractions (most of which are also habits, btw), which means you can be an expert at anticipating your excuses and distractions and head them off at the pass.

If you're making writing for an hour every morning into a new habit, for example, and you know that drifting off into the captivating and endless world of online shoe shopping is your jam, turn off the internet for that hour. As in go downstairs and unplug it (it's too easy to just turn it on and off on your computer). If you're giving up meat and you drive past your favorite rib joint on your way home from work every day, take a different route. If you're serious about learning the clarinet and you know you can't resist the charms of puttering in your garden, take your clarinet to a park/a friend's house/a practice space or sit in your car and run your scales there. There are so very many simple ways to avoid the things, people, situations, activities, wafts of smoking pork that derail you, so use your valuable insider info and get proactive. And while you're at it, don't feel gross or self-loathing or ashamed of how intimately you know your excuses and past failures and weak spots; they're simply another part of who you are and part of what makes you an interesting person. Be grateful that you're on such intimate terms with your escape hatches, because now you can move some heavy furniture on top of them while you head out to kick some butt.

Get your notebook, think about the habit you're working on, and write down every single thing you can think of that you'll use to throw a banana peel in your path—screwing around on Twitter, suddenly making a lasagna, running errands, doing the dishes, brushing the dog, dusting off your lighting fixtures, alphabetizing your spice drawer—and block your ability to participate.

Please also make a list of the people in your life who may be too partylicious to be around while you give up drinking and drugs, too pessimistic to hang out with while you do your part to help end world hunger, too gossipy to chat with while you quit gossiping, too small-minded to be around while you get your new business off the ground—and make a point to limit your time with them.

I also want you to once again sit in the feeling of eager expectation around your new habit and write down any objections that come up. We all have tried-and-true arguments that we use over and over to knock ourselves off track, so along with your mantra, come up with a one-liner that will put your most familiar excuse in its place. For example:

I've tried going vegan a million times and it never sticks. = Those times were practice; this is the real deal.

I have no willpower, who am I kidding? = We've put a man on the Moon. I can do this. I can do anything.

I don't really care about getting in shape. I'm out! = I love my body, I love myself, and I love feeling good.

I don't need to meditate/work out/floss/make a gratitude list every day. Once in a while is good. = This goes way beyond this habit. It's about being in control of my life, my happiness, my way of showing up in the world.

This isn't doing anything/is taking forever. I give up. = Successful people never give up. I deserve success. I am doing this.

Please say your mantra right now. Say it out loud, say it to yourself, say it all day long. Feel it, see it, love it, believe it, rejoice in it, become it, repeat it, and then repeat it some more. Say it right before you fall asleep and first thing when you wake up.

DAY 7: REWARD YOURSELF

Habits with instant results are easier to stick to than the habits that seem to take forever to make any difference. Brushing your teeth, for example, immediately makes your mouth feel fresh and clean, so it's easy to do it on a daily basis. Flossing your teeth is more of a slog, however, because what do you walk away with after flossing? The occasional bloody gum? Not exactly a big draw.

When our brains anticipate or experience pleasure, they release the cracklike chemical called dopamine. We become addicted to that sweet dopamine rush (I don't know about you but I go to sleep some nights fantasizing about the cup of coffee I get to have the next morning), and we look forward to the habits, both good and bad, that come with some zing attached. Unfortunately, most of the habits we're trying to adopt around here don't really knock it out of the park in the dopamine department, or else we'd most likely already be participating in them;

so in order to keep ourselves engaged, we have to get creative. One great way to make even the most ho-hum of habits something to look forward to is by attaching some sort of reward to it.

Think about your habit and come up with something you can entice yourself with while you're actively doing it, or that you can look forward to after you've success-fully accomplished it, or stayed away from it, as the case may be. All things that bring you pleasure are game, even guilty little pleasures—we're going for the gold here, so do whatever it takes as long as it's not illegal, harmful to yourself or others, or counterproductive (eating a tub of ice cream isn't the best reward for sticking to your diet, for example).

Here are some suggestions I've collected from habit-forming superstars that will hopefully inspire you to come up with a compelling insta-treat for the long haul. Once you've decided how you'll be rewarding yourself, write down the details of what you'll do and commit to treat-ing yourself every single time you perform, or stay away from, your habit.

- When you sit down to eat your healthy, low-cal meal, then and only then can you check your social media.

- After writing for two hours each morning . . . chocolate.

- Get an accountability buddy who's also on a quest to go to the spiritual gym each morning (meditating, journaling, studying self-help books). Send each other an email the night before with a love note, a quote, a quick encouragement, an inspiring article, or a video of a cat eating a bag of potato chips—you get to open the email only after you've successfully shown up at the spiritual gym the next morning.

- After a cigarette-free day, you get to masturbate. Otherwise, can't touch this.

- After you swim your laps, stop off and play with the puppies at the pound on your way home from the pool.

- Watch the next episode of your favorite bingeworthy show only while running on the treadmill.

- Find a friend who's on a quest to build her business too. You each get points for the number of sales calls you make each day. At the end of the week, whoever has the most points takes the other out for dinner.

- After successfully participating in your "stranger-a-day" commitment to flirting with one new hot person per day, blast your favorite song and think about how hot and sexy and lovable you are.

- After an entire day of successfully not complaining, take a hot bath with all your fancy bath salts and candles and perhaps a barricade in front of the door so your kids can't get in and disturb you.

• •

Please say your mantra right now. Say it out loud, say it to yourself, say it all day long. Feel it, see it, love it, believe it, rejoice in it, become it, repeat it, and then repeat it some more. Say it right before you fall asleep and first thing when you wake up.

• •

DAY 8: SURROUND YOURSELF WITH GREATNESS, HUMAN AND OTHERWISE.

When I was seven years old, we took our first big family trip to my dad's hometown of Naples, Italy. The majority of our relatives still lived in the cluster of houses where my dad grew up, a compound of sorts built into the side of a mountain overlooking the Bay of Naples. The experience of flying across the ocean in a plane with two decks (hello!), getting to stay up as late as we wanted every night (hello again!), and tasting my first sip of wine (disgusting), offered to me by a woman (my aunt) who looked just like my dad (same huge nose), was staggering. But the thing that really blew my tiny mind was my nonno's chicken coop. Right there, on the edge of the communal Sincero vegetable garden, was a little henhouse complete with roosts for the birds to sleep on, a tiny fenced-in yard, and a nesting box where they laid eggs that rolled down a ramp and into a padded crate. I sat in that stinky hut and stared at that crate, motionless, for hours each day, waiting for a hot, blue egg to magically appear, and then I'd run screaming up to the house waving it over my head like a live snake. I could not believe my parents never told me: Regular people can have chickens. Real chickens that lay real eggs. Regular. People. Like. Me.

Immediately upon our return home I found the perfect place in our yard for a coop (shady, far from the swing set so they wouldn't be disturbed, visible from my bedroom window so I could keep a twenty-four-hour watch). I spoke of nothing else, drew and redrew plans for the structure, and after endless tearful and persistent negotiations, my parents finally brushed me off with a barely acceptable "Fine, when you're fourteen you can have a chicken coop." They were, of course, counting on the fact that I'd lose interest by then, and foolishly scoffed at my threat to take legal action if they didn't honor the contract that I wrote up and made them sign.

The fact that my parents were correct and I ended up being more interested in boys than chickens by age fourteen is beside the point. I spent the next few years obsessed with all things raising chickens, wrote a paper for my Earth Science class on the endlessly fascinating cloaca (one hole, so many jobs!), and made a chicken coop diorama that hung above the fish tank in our playroom for years.

Having that experience in Italy woke me up to possibilities and parts of myself that I didn't know existed before then, which is why I will now encourage you to be very aware of, and proactive about, the environments you put yourself in whilst cultivating your new habit.

> We are enormously influenced by who and what we surround ourselves with; our environment can make or break us faster than almost anything.

If you want to stop gambling and you hang out at Gamblers Anonymous meetings, for example, you're much more likely to be successful than if you try to stop gambling and still hang out with poker obsessives and/or at casinos. No duh, right, but . . . how are you hanging? If you want to be happier and more optimistic, hang out with happy, optimistic people and pay attention to how they speak, think, perceive the world, and react when the stray dog they picked up along the highway chews a hole in their car seat. If you want to get into the habit of doing something every day to help the planet, put recycling bins next to all the garbage cans in your house, go to and listen to lectures on climate change, volunteer at your local community garden, or join a park pickup day. Insert yourself in any environmentally conscious environment where you can not only help out but where you can be around like-minded people who will give you even more ideas on how you can make a difference.

Remember, you want to make your good habits easy to participate in and your bad habits a pain in the butt, and making smart choices about your environment is one of the most effective ways to do this.

Because we're only interested in you succeeding at your habit, and not at all interested in you succeeding at being overwhelmed, please start by picking one aspect of your surroundings in each of the four environments below and commit to upgrading it. If you have the time and enthusiasm to do more, go for it, but start with making one change in each area. And please write down the changes you're going to make, include the details of who, what, where, and when, and then go make it happen.

YOUR HUMAN ENVIRONMENT

Pick a stellar human being who is currently where you desire to be in regard to your habit (or beyond) and hang out with them on a regular basis; become accountability partners; or hire them as a personal trainer, a coach, a workout buddy, someone who guards your refrigerator and sounds a bullhorn every time you open the door. Or take a class, join a support group, or go to a seminar and make as many connections as possible. Extra credit: While you're upgrading your posse, limit your exposure to people who will knock you off track, tempt you to stray, or throw a wet blanket on your enthusiasm. You know who they are. Tell them you're really busy.

YOUR PHYSICAL ENVIRONMENT

Hang up pictures that remind you of the body you're working toward, the trip you'll take when you make the money, the soul mate you're calling in, the mountain you'll climb when you're in shape, the candidate you'll help get elected. Go test-drive the car you'll buy, walk through the part of town you'll live in, stare at the marquee that your name will be on, strut around in the cowboy boots you'll buy and strike a pose for everyone in the shoe store. Clear out a space to exercise in, to meditate in, to paint in. You want your surroundings to mirror back to you the kind of person you're becoming, so make them as inspiring, welcoming, and good-looking as possible.

YOUR SPIRITUAL ENVIRONMENT

Join a meditation group, listen to guided meditations, read inspiring books, do kirtan, yoga, or transcendental meditation. Take at least five minutes every day to get quiet and go inward. Silence your mind and sink into the understanding that you are a hugely powerful creature able to make manifest anything you set your mind to. Breathe. Shut yer piehole. Imagine light running down through your head and out your feet. Allow the Universe to flow through you. Get your doubts, fears, and negative self-talk out of the way. Taking five minutes every single day to connect to your higher self can make all the difference in the world.

YOUR EMOTIONAL ENVIRONMENT

Listen to music that pumps you up and makes you happy. Read, watch, participate in, and listen to things that make you laugh, give you big ideas, boost your confidence, educate you, inspire the crap out of you, fill you with joy, put a skip in your step. Surround yourself with pictures of the people in your life who love you. Do things that feel good to your body, talk about yourself and others fondly, hang out with people you love, pet cute animals, walk around in nature, ponder the sky, surround yourself with things and people and sounds and smells and tastes and sights that delight you and build your confidence.

• •

Please say your mantra right now. Say it out loud, say it to yourself, say it all day long. Feel it, see it, love it, believe it, rejoice in it, become it, repeat it, and then repeat it some more. Say it right before you fall asleep and first thing when you wake up.

• •

DAY 9: CREATE A RITUAL

I went to college with this guy named Dave. One day I walked into his dorm room to find him sitting at his desk all dressed up in a suit and tie, shiny shoes, hair just so, maybe even some cuff links. He had a bunch of open textbooks in front of him and appeared to be studying. I instantly chastised myself for not knocking, as this was clearly a private, odd, and awkward moment, but Dave was unfazed. "I've got a big economics test tomorrow," he explained. "I find I focus better if I get dressed up. You gotta look good to be good!" I was utterly blown away by such an advanced and respectable commitment to success. Especially since I no doubt had a big test the next day too and was probably there to buy pot from his roommate.

Ritual is an ancient and powerful practice used to pray, give thanks, and mark such important milestones as weddings, deaths, quinceañeras, harvest seasons, bat and bar mitzvahs, full moons, high tides, and, according to Dave, big economics tests. Rituals bring purpose, renewal, ceremony, and celebration to our lives and can be very helpful to you as you hone your habit. For starters, rituals can help you focus on and engage more deeply with what you're doing. One of the reasons some people light a candle when they sit down to meditate is because it marks the beginning of an important event, pulls their focus toward what they're about to do, and acknowledges their forthcoming conversation with the almighty Universe as the big fat deal that it is. Without lighting the candle, they might be tempted to just plop on down in the middle of a busy day with this thought in the back of their mind: *Welp, I may make it through the whole twenty minutes of meditating, I may not.* The candle represents commitment, focus, respect, not screwing around.

Rituals around our habits also act as nods of appreciation. They communicate that we're taking ourselves and our commitments seriously. It doesn't matter if your goal is to stop burping out loud or if you're taking daily steps to help end human trafficking; you must consciously honor the fact that you're showing up for yourself and that this is a sacred act.

> The more you appreciate yourself, the more likely you are to stick to habits that are good for you and lose the ones that aren't.

I've heard that Tom Cruise has a ritual of beating his chest and hollering about how awesome he is before he goes on camera, to psych himself up. Some families hold hands and say grace before eating to show thanks. Certain Native American tribes perform dances to call for rain. My dog sits at my feet, solemnly bows his head, places a paw on my knee, and prays to the God of Walks.

Here are some examples of rituals to help inspire you to come up with the perfect one for you and your habit:

- If you're getting into shape, look at your body in the mirror before your workout, appreciate all it does for you, and thank it for its faithful service all these years.

- If you're studying French every day for an hour, make a special cup of coffee or tea or pour a glass of juice to mark the beginning of your session. After you take your first sip, say out loud "Je suis amaze-balls."

- If you're getting into the habit of being more present, every time you sit down to eat, pay attention to each bite of food you take, chew slowly and taste all the flavors, feel the nutrients nourishing your body when you swallow, and be tearfully grateful that you have the great gift of food to feed yourself and the teeth to chew it with.

- If you're quitting smoking, take three deep breaths every morning and visualize your happy, healthy lungs getting even happier and healthier. Do this also when you get a craving.

- If you're making a habit of being more loving and appreciative of your partner, put on a bracelet, a pair of earrings, or a watch each morning to acknowledge your open heart, your gratitude for all the amazing things they bring to your life, and your intention to love them like they ain't never been loved before.

- If you're walking to work every day with a friend, come up with a special handshake you greet each other with that acknowledges your commitment to your health and your friendship.

- If you're quitting the habit of biting your nails, move a ring from one hand to the other each morning to announce a new day of victory.

- If you're getting into the habit of becoming more aware, kind, and compassionate, carry a special rock in your pocket to remind yourself to connect with your heart.

- If you're getting into the habit of writing a gratitude list every morning or evening, sit down slowly, feel your butt hitting the chair, and recognize that your body is presently on a planet whizzing through infinite space and that you are about to harness the profound power of gratitude with your magic pen.

Saying your mantra every day is also a ritual. Let's go ahead and do that right now.

DAY 10: FOCUS LIKE A FIEND

Many moons ago when I lived in Manhattan, a friend of mine and I were sitting on a park bench eating lunch. We were so busy talking that we didn't notice the alarm that was going off at the bank right across the street from us, and it wasn't until the noise suddenly stopped, after blaring away for a good fifteen minutes, that we finally came to and thought, *Wow, it's so nice and quiet!* We were so used to noise and chaos that the silence was more alarming to us than the alarm. That was the moment I realized, *You know, I reckon it's about time I moved out of the city.*

We get into the unconscious habit of accepting thoughts and beliefs that literally cause us alarm, hold us back, and make us feel terrible about ourselves. We treat these thoughts and beliefs as if they're the truth—*I'm a fraud; I'm unlovable; My memory sucks; I'll always be overweight; Nobody listens to me; I have a face like a foot*—until we come to and realize, *Hey, wait a minute, these beliefs stink. I have the power of choice. I'm gonna train my focus on beliefs and thoughts that bring me joy, success, and peace instead.*

As discussed in Chapter 1, what you focus on you create more of, so as you master your new habit, it's important to adjust and strengthen the mighty lens of your conscious mind to make sure it's serving you well. This is why we're dedicating today, all day, to sharpening the profoundly transformational tool known as your focus. All day today, be a helicopter parent to your brain and strictly monitor what you tune in to. Tie a string around your wrist, draw an eye on the back of your hand, put notes all over your house to remind yourself that today is the high holy day of positive focus, and:

1. **Commit to finding things in your environment that reinforce your new identity.** For example, choose to notice all the different kinds of people who are in great shape if you're starting a habit of regularly working out. If you're getting into the habit of being in a healthy relationship, be on the lookout for happy, loving couples. If you're quitting dairy, zero in on all the incredible dairy-free options in the supermarket, as well as all the other delicious foods that don't involve dairy that you get to eat. If you're getting in the habit of saying only good things about yourself, notice all the reasons you're so staggeringly special and really hear and digest the

compliments other people give to you. Or if you're giving up junk food, revel in the glory that is a perfectly ripe peach. Build a new foundation of proof that this habit of yours is possible, available, and basically stalking you right now.

2. **Focus on the fact that you're doing yourself a favor rather than feeling like you're denying yourself something.** For example, instead of focusing on how you'd love to lie in bed all morning, acknowledge how much you're improving your life by getting up early to walk before work. Instead of getting caught up in your craving for bread, be proud of yourself for dodging the bloating that haunts your relationship with wheat. In order to refrain from explaining to your bestie, in colorful detail, what a chowderhead your stereo-blasting, nocturnal neighbor is, celebrate your choice to talk about meaningful things, not the jackassery of others, during your precious time with her. Think about all the pluses of participating in your new habit, write them down, and notice what a great friend you're being to yourself.

3. **Make a section in your notebook where you'll keep track of how it feels when you enjoy your habit, and be on the lookout today for these moments.** No matter how dull going through the motions of your habit may seem, there will be times when it's enjoyable. When

I meditate, for example, I sometimes feel a twinge of excitement in my gut: *Holy crap, I'm hanging with the big guy!* When flossing my teeth, I realize that I'm cleaning them, that I'm a good person who cares about her gums, that I've trained myself to do something that's boring . . . and it feels good. I tend to feel excitement in the base of my stomach, and I want you to figure out not only where you connect physically to the emotion of joy but what thoughts are running through your head when joy happens in relation to your habit. Write down the specifics in your notebook and call up these details—run the words through your head and put a hand on the place in your body—before or while you participate in your habit. This will help you stay the course when you really don't feel like it, and the more you repeat this exercise, the more automatically you'll associate the feelings of joy and anticipation, instead of boredom/dread/laziness, with your habit.

4. **Pull back and focus on the bigger picture.** It's so easy to get caught up in the drama and minutiae of our lives, but we always have the choice to see things from a more expansive, far more profound viewpoint. If you found out your best friend hooked up with your boyfriend or girlfriend, for example, you'd probably stew on it rather animatedly for a long while. But let's say that at the peak

of your stewing you narrowly escaped a shark attack or somehow survived a plane crash—suddenly you'd see things from a different perspective and your romantic situation wouldn't be such a big fat deal anymore. Your gratitude for simply being alive would take center stage, and images of the two of them naked in bed together, while understandably unappealing and painful, would start fading into the background. Luckily, you don't have to suffer a harrowing experience to pull back and appreciate your life; you just have to remember to make the choice. Widen your scope and appreciate that this day-to-day habit exercise isn't just about this one day but rather that it affects your whole life. All your good habits add up to you being the best version of yourself.

Please say your mantra right now. Say it out loud, say it to yourself, say it all day long. Feel it, see it, love it, believe it, rejoice in it, become it, repeat it, and then repeat it some more. Say it right before you fall asleep and first thing when you wake up.

DAY 11: TAKE TINY BITES

When I'm writing something large and lengthy, I have this bananas habit of stopping myself right when I realize that the words are rolling and I'm in the flow—I immediately stand up and get a cup of coffee; check my email; decide I should learn to play the trumpet, right now; clean out my garage; or build a tree house. It's Self-Sabotage 101, but thankfully I'm aware of it, so I've learned to keep my need to distract myself in its cage by chunking down my time. I set an alarm for twenty minutes on my phone and during that time I'm unauthorized to get up and pee, snack, check a text, doodle a doodle, basically do anything other than write, no matter how much I squirm. Then I take a little break. Then I set the timer for another twenty minutes. Sometimes, once I've calmed myself down and proven that I won't burst into flames if I focus on writing, I start upping my time chunks to twenty-five minutes, thirty minutes, etc. Sometimes I stick with twenty-minute chunks all day long. It's not the size of the chunks that matters, it's the fact that I take them seriously and refuse to budge. And taking a break isn't mandatory, btw; if I'm in the flow, I keep writing past my chunked-out time, *OMG check it out, I'm still writing and I don't even have to be. How is this even happening?!*

I know that if I start treating my time chunks as anything less than what they are—the collective building blocks of my entire reality—and allow even the weensiest excuse to squeak its way in and squander my minutes, I am screwed.

> All the little moments in our lives add up to the whole of who we are.

Our tiny moments decide if we're generally successful or unsuccessful, if we're healthy or unhealthy, if we're happy or unhappy, if we sit down to write an entire book or merely eke out a helpful pamphlet. Get into the habit of treating the stepping-stones to your success like the great leaps forward that they are if you want to find yourself standing in a reality you're extremely psyched about. Plus, come on, twenty minutes—how hard is it to do anything for twenty minutes?

Our dear sweet brains go into overwhelm so easily, especially when we set out to make positive changes in our lives. Why does it seem like there's always so much to DO? *On top of all the things I'm already doing, now I have to journal and focus and say my mantra and lay out my clothes and haul my ass to the gym on time every day?* Adopting new habits can seem daunting, especially if you're going for something that's really shifting a way of being that you've been participating in for the majority of your life. This is why the practice of taking things one day at a time is so magnificent and liberating: It takes the drama of forever out of the equation and allows us to more softly put aside old ways of being as opposed to dramatically chopping them off. It also allows us to step back and practice imperfection, process, and patience by acknowledging that change takes time. You will have good days, and you will have bad days; the key is to stay focused on the good and to forgive the bad.

Take a moment now to think about your habit and come up with a way to shrink it down into a tiny, bite-sized task or chunk of time. Here are a few examples to help spark some ideas:

- Sit and write just one page of your book.

- Swim just one mile this morning.

- Practice piano for just five minutes. Next time you sit down do it for seven minutes. Then ten.

- Say not one bad thing about anyone throughout your entire lunch date with your friends.

- Do just ten sit-ups. Next time do twelve, then fifteen.

- Make just three sales calls before getting up from your desk.

- Refrain from cursing just for today.

- Floss your teeth just this morning.

- Leave your phone in the cupboard just for tonight while you enjoy dinner with your family.

Please say your mantra right now. Say it out loud, say it to yourself, say it all day long. Feel it, see it, love it, believe it, rejoice in it, become it, repeat it, and then repeat it some more. Say it right before you fall asleep and first thing when you wake up.

DAY 12: TAME YOUR TRIGGERS

On Day 5 we discussed becoming unavailable to participate in negotiations. Today we're going to take that one step further by not only refusing to negotiate but by using the negotiations to trigger a positive activity or thought. Now the urge to negotiate will go from being a negative temptation to a positive reminder.

For example, when the craving for a cookie seizes you, use your desire to negotiate, or to indulge in an exception, as a cue to drink a big glass of water. When you start negotiating about blowing off your morning meditation, use your squirminess as a reminder to say your mantra five times before sitting your butt down to meditate. Instead of opting out of your volunteer gig as a reading tutor, use your longing to be lazy to reinforce your commitment; use the impulse to call in sick as a trigger to conjure up a mental image of the excited little faces on the kids when a new word sinks in and they suddenly "get it." When you're gripped by the temptation to stand by the cheese platter at a party and pop cheddar cubes into your mouth, visualize your unwanted weight melting off your body. If the urge to make a self-deprecating joke comes up, pay someone a compliment, yourself included.

They key is to have a specific replacement in mind so that when, not if, you're tempted to stray, you're ready. Come up with a positive activity or thought, write it down in your notebook, and whip it out the next time a negotiation has the audacity to approach you and your habit. You have a choice as to how you receive whatever input comes your way. Make the conscious decision to use your triggers as positive reminders, not as habit killers.

· ·

Please say your mantra right now. Say it out loud, say it to yourself, say it all day long. Feel it, see it, love it, believe it, rejoice in it, become it, repeat it, and then repeat it some more. Say it right before you fall asleep and first thing when you wake up.

· ·

DAY 13: REMEMBER TO REMEMBER

Today we're celebrating the fact that you're more than halfway to completing your 21 days by taking a moment to remember what a powerful creature you are. Let's start by appreciating what you've accomplished over these past few weeks: You've shown up over and over again; you've learned about your strengths and weaknesses; you've gotten specific about your desires, thoughts, and actions; you've opened yourself up to failure; you've positioned yourself for success; you've taken responsibility for your own happiness; you've decided to create what you want; you've cast asunder your tried-and-true excuses; you've gotten uncomfy; and you've shown that you believe in yourself and love yourself enough to do what it takes to change your life.

> You can literally accomplish anything you set your mind to. It doesn't matter how many times you've messed up, because your failures and face-plants are all part of your journey.

You get to choose whether you perceive your mistakes as proof that you're a moron or proof that you're in the game or proof that you had a lesson to learn or proof that you're growing or proof that you stuck with it anyway or proof that you're never gonna let that happen again. You understand that where you choose to place your focus determines how you perceive your reality, and while you sometimes lose sight of this truth, you're getting better and better at remaining aware.

Remember that your desires were given to you because they're meant for you. Remember that you were given the means to make manifest these desires by believing in the not yet seen, by focusing your thoughts and words on the hollerings of your heart instead of on your fears, by surrounding yourself with extraordinary people, by consciously shifting your habits to align with who you're becoming, and by repeatedly taking action that makes you groan a bit.

You are part of an infinite Universe—you are mighty and magnificent, and to think that you can't or shouldn't or don't deserve the desires that light up your heart is as ridiculous as a tree thinking it shouldn't grow or the sun thinking it shouldn't set or a sheep thinking it shouldn't bleat.

> When you step it up and decide to create awesome habits, you are reminding yourself (literally resetting your mind) of who you truly are.

You are here to blossom into the most authentic, joyful, bright, shiny version of yourself, and by doing this you not only live a far more merry life than you would sad-sacking away in the shadows but you shine light on everyone in your orbit. By being your best self, you light a fuse within others, inspire them, and show them what's possible for them too.

Congratulations. A million thanks. Please keep the torch lit.

● ●

Please say your mantra right now. Say it out loud, say it to yourself, say it all day long. Feel it, see it, love it, believe it, rejoice in it, become it, repeat it, and then repeat it some more. Say it right before you fall asleep and first thing when you wake up.

● ●

DAY 14: SPEAK IT INTO BEING

Anyone who thinks words aren't powerful never knew my high school basketball coach. She could talk anyone into anything, including my six-foot-tall, basketball-hating freshman self into being on her varsity team. As someone who excelled at being neither popular nor coordinated, I was terrified to be around those older girls while putting my gangly lack of athletic ability on display. My skill for accidentally bouncing the ball off my sneaker and shooting at the wrong basket was of no concern to my coach, however. All she saw was a girl human with octopus arms who was taller than most of Westchester County. Adult men included.

"Rebound and pass. Do not dribble, do not shoot, just get the ball and pass it. You're our secret weapon, Sincero, you will make us state champions!" Her pep talks also included such intoxicating words as "star," "special," and "pizza parties," so in spite of my excruciating shin splints and the new nicknames that I knew my unlikely sports career would inspire from my bullies (Lurch, Gigantore, Sigmund the Sea Monster), I spent the better part of my freshman year loping up and down the basketball court in my ill-fitting uniform, my bulbous knees knocking together on my skinny legs like coconuts.

I somehow managed to make it through the entire season, and I might have let her sucker me into joining the following year had she not completely blown her credibility by convincing me, against my protests, that it would be a great idea to dress up as Big Bird for Field Day. Suffice it to say, towering over my costumed class-mates as we marched onto the football field wearing nothing but bright yellow tights, a leotard covered in feathers, and a beak fashioned out of a traffic cone was not something my tenuous social status could withstand. Having officially reached my threshold for humiliation, I finally became immune to my ex-coach's advances, and the varsity girls' basketball team wound up two coconuts short of making it to state the next year.

I've also been talked into buying a gigantic television that I neither needed nor wanted; I convinced my little sister that my parents adopted her from the scary, drunk guy who hung out on the deli wall in town; and most of us have, at least once in our lives, gone into a salon for a trim and left with a mortifying hairdo that the pushy hairdresser insisted would look fabulous.

> Watch your words. And everyone else's.

Your words anchor in your reality, so if you talk about how lazy you are or how much you suck at remembering people's birthdays or how you love love love that cigarette with your coffee or how you have no willpower, so it shall be. Today I'd like you to focus on the words that come out of your mouth and that roll around in your head. Again, if you need a visual cue to jar you out of robotic thinking mode, tie a string around your wrist or leave notes around your house or put a sticker on your phone—whatever helps you remember that today, yer all about the werd.

You've been saying your mantra every day. How else can you employ words to support the new you? Well, I'll tell you. Start by getting into the headspace once again of the person you're becoming and imagine yourself speaking as they would speak all day long, like you're a hand puppet on the end of their arm. *What would my habit hero say?* Then please do the following:

- **Be on the lookout for the following phrases:**

   I can't

   I wish

   I want

   I will

   I suck at

   I'm trying to

   I hate

   And replace them with these phrases:

   I love

   I can

   I do

   I am

   I create

   I excel at

   I'm so grateful I

- **Notice any habitual ways of speaking and thinking that don't represent the big, badass new you and knock that shit off.** And while you're at it, replace the negativity with opposing, empowering words and thoughts.

- **Using the powerful phrases listed above, write down three things that the person you're becoming would say and find a way to use those phrases today.** Extra points if the phrases contradict something the old you would say.

- **Be intentional about the words you receive.** If you're exposed to any toxic, icky, or bullying words that might throw you off track, turn off the television, put down the paper, close the document, remove yourself, ignore it, or if you're stuck in the presence of a negative blowhard, drown them out by repeating your mantra over and over in your head.

· ·

Please say your mantra right now. Say it out loud, say it to yourself, say it all day long. Feel it, see it, love it, believe it, rejoice in it, become it, repeat it, and then repeat it some more. Say it right before you fall asleep and first thing when you wake up.

· ·

DAY 15: CULTIVATE YOUR CONFIDENCE

Confidence means to confide in yourself, to trust in your own strength and smarts, to believe that *I got this*. Even when you kinda don't really know what the hell you're doing, you still have confidence that you'll figure it out. When it comes to bringing healthy new habits into your life, you must have confidence in your ability to succeed or else the complainers and the doubters and the couch cushions and the smoking sections and the donut shops of the world will swallow you up—and all your best intentions right along with you.

The good news is that you were born confident. Confidence isn't something you need to go out and get; it's already who you are. You just need to move your unhelpful thoughts out of the way and let your true self come blazing through.

> Any fears, doubts, or worries you have about yourself and your fabulousness were learned from the people around you and from your own temporary failures. They are not the truth.

I suck at yoga; I can't sing; I have a horrible temper; I'm a slob—all of these are simply beliefs, and one way to shift these beliefs is by bolstering your confidence, which is what we're going to do today.

Here are some of my favorite tips for boosting your belief in your badass self:

1. **Let your body lead your mind.** Our minds and our bodies are total BFFs. They're in constant communication; they share everything and love nothing more than being samesies. When our minds are full of stress and dark thoughts, for example, our bodies commiserate by filling with dis-ease, getting headaches, picking at cuticles, feeling faint and stumbling around, clinging to furniture. When our minds are happy and full of hope, we have energy, glowing skin, big dopey grins, and high fives for

everyone. Conversely, if our bodies get hit by a car or bitten by a snake, our minds fill with fear, sadness, and desperation, and if we're in shape, well-fed, and wearing super-cute shoes, we feel happy, sexy, and invincible.

All day today, adopt the body language of a confident person and your malleable mind will follow suit: walk tall, sit up straight, smile, breathe slowly and deeply, push your shoulders back, and stand with your feet shoulder-width apart. Controlling your posture is one of the simplest and most powerful ways to strengthen your confidence, so please really do this and notice how much mightier you feel.

2. **Act as if you're confident.** Revisit this idea of acting like the person you're becoming and focus on the fact that you're oozing confidence. Throughout the day today, and especially right before you practice your new habit, or disengage from your old habit, imagine yourself in your new, fully confident identity. You're so self-assured, worry-free, matter-of-fact, poised, and in control that you barely even register the habit at all. *Of course I'm going for a run; it's what I do and I do it well. What plate of warm cookies? All I see is my sunny kitchen and my adorable kids gathered around the table having a snack. I don't even remember struggling to meditate, it's so*

second nature to me. You mean to tell me that people actually struggle with it? Create a character out of the confident person you're becoming and strut around in their fancypants all day long.

3. **Compile proof.** Get your notebook and write down three instances in your past when you overcame your doubts and proved that you could do something. Write down anything from getting the job you didn't think you could get to dating someone out of your league to taking the trip on your bucket list to moving your entire family across the country to beating your neighbor Billy "the Brain" McClain at chess. Three. Write them down. See? You're already confident.

4. **Practice.** Build your confidence muscle bit by bit by taking tiny actions. If you're adopting the habit of being a better salesperson, practice by selling your kids on the many advantages of going to bed on time. If you're getting into the habit of being a better listener, spend the first five minutes of your next conversation with a stranger offering nothing but eye contact, understanding nods, and investigative questions. If you're getting into the habit of being more outgoing, practice smiling and making eye contact with yourself in the mirror. The key is to practice in a safe space, where the outcome isn't hugely loaded, and to do things that push you

outside your comfort zone but not completely off the cliff. Come up with three little practice activities to build your confidence and do them today.

5. **Make it about serving others.** When it comes to lacking confidence, the most common culprits that keep us down are fear of looking stupid, being rejected, and losing everything we've got (money, dignity, friends, jobs, self-respect). Which is why taking the focus off yourself and instead making your quest for confidence all about what you can offer other people is so powerful. One of the best pieces of advice I ever got, from a speaking coach who was helping me with debilitating nerves before getting onstage, was to see myself as a conduit for the information I was meant to deliver (rather than as someone who was in desperate need of approval). I would, of course, do my best, but it was none of my business whether or not the audience thought I was amazing or a total yo-yo. My job was just to deliver the information as best I could.

Stand tall as the you that you're becoming and imagine the gifts you're meant to give flowing out through your fingertips, the confident energy radiating out of your body, powerful words spilling forth from your mouth. See yourself as a conduit for the mighty messages the Universe needs your fellow earthlings to receive, and picture all the people you will help by improving yourself.

6. **Surround yourself with cheerleaders.** As discussed on Day 8, your environment greatly affects your perception of yourself, of what you believe is possible, and of how easy or difficult it will be to refrain from drinking beer for breakfast. Your environment also greatly affects your ability to remain confident, so please be aware of what you've got going on and upgrade where necessary. Read inspiring books; hang out with like-minded people who think you're brilliant and hilarious; don't hang out with people who can't see your glory or in places that will derail you, bring you down, or offer you free cookies with your salad. Listen to, look at, eat, wear, and participate in things that make you feel happy and confident; the more consciously you design your surroundings to bolster your confidence, the more confident you will be.

7. **Remember: Nobody really knows what the hell they're doing.** Are some people generally more confident than others? Sure. Does everybody have an Achilles' heel of insecurity? You betcha. I can't tell you how many people have said to me, while trading stories of being in high school, "I had friends but I didn't really belong to any one group. I was an outsider." We've all been honing

feelings of less-than for decades, but I am here to tell you that even some of the popular kids in high school, yes, even Tiffany Fanucci, whom I bumped into last time I was in my hometown, have confessed to feeling like outsiders.

It's easy to think that everyone else is much more together, more confident, happier, or taking better vacations than we are (thank you, social media), when in reality we're all winging it to some degree. This is not to say life's a competition or a game of comparison; I'm a fan of neither. I just want to remind you that nobody has it all figured out. Yourself included. So don't hold your sweet self to an impossible standard. Instead please appreciate the unique individual that you are and enjoy the learning process that is your one and only life.

• •

Please say your mantra right now. Say it out loud, say it to yourself, say it all day long. Feel it, see it, love it, believe it, rejoice in it, become it, repeat it, and then repeat it some more. Say it right before you fall asleep and first thing when you wake up.

• •

DAY 16: BOOK IT

Have you ever charmed your way into a job with no prior experience, immediately panicked—*I have no idea what the hell I'm doing. These poor people are paying me! Can I go to jail for this?*—and then figured things out as you went along? Or have you ever booked a trip with no idea how you'll find the money to pay for it or the time to go, only to find yourself sunning on a white sand beach a few months later, cocktail and selfie stick in hand, after stubbornly making the time and money present themselves? Or have you ever had a report due, blown it off for weeks, sat down to fake-write it day after day, clocked in more hours than you care to admit freaking out, complaining to friends, quietly weeping in the fetal position, only to crank it out the night before with flying colors? When we're faced with deadlines, ultimatums, the option to sink or swim, even if we can't see any real way to stay afloat, most of us eventually figure out how to keep our heads above water.

> There are few better accountability partners than panic, nonrefundable expense, and the threat of public humiliation.

Today's assignment is to put something in place that will hold you accountable for sticking to your habit. If you're starting a habit of jogging every morning, for example, sign up for a marathon that you will proudly train for and complete, and make sure to tell all your friends to save the date so they can make T-shirts with your face on them and cheer you through the finish line. If you're learning piano, book a gig to perform at a friend's party or at a club or on Facebook Live. Throw yourself a big anniversary party celebrating six months of no smoking—send out the invites, put down the nonrefundable deposit on the band that will play, ask for the time off from work. Celebrate thirty days of uninterrupted Pilates classes by buying tickets to an Ice Capades performance happening a month from now.

Come up with some future sort of something and spend today booking it, buying it, and inviting all your friends to it, and let the deadline work its harrowing magic of holding you to your habit.

Please say your mantra right now. Say it out loud, say it to yourself, say it all day long. Feel it, see it, love it, believe it, rejoice in it, become it, repeat it, and then repeat it some more. Say it right before you fall asleep and first thing when you wake up.

DAY 17: GIVE THANKS

I could write volumes on the power of gratitude, but today I'm going to focus on how it can help you stick to your habit and inspire you to become the kind of person you're ready to be. As discussed, in every single moment you have a choice as to where you place your focus and how you act, and the key to firing up this almighty power of choice is awareness.

Take a moment now and look back on your life: Was there ever a situation that made you think something along the lines of *Damn, I wish I'd let myself have more fun in high school instead of feeling so dumpy and insecure and terminally undatable*? Or have you ever gotten yourself all worked up, spun out, and stomachachy over a conversation you were terrified to have or a move you were scared to make, only to have it turn out to be no big whoop-de-do? And can you imagine how incredible it would have been in those scenarios to have placed your focus on all that you had to be grateful for instead of on fear and loathing? Yes, in the midst of life's many mucky moments, we experience fun-free feelings, chaos, and the humiliating results of our terrible choices. But imagine if you were able to feel all the things and struggle with the struggles and learn the hard lessons without forgetting that you may also choose appreciation and gratitude and grace.

> Gratitude isn't about denying your difficult feelings; it's about not being a prisoner to them.

Making room for both gratitude and grouchiness is like looking in the mirror, unenthusiastically taking in all the wrinkles on your face, and then remembering to remember that you'll never be this young again; you don't have to pretend that you love how your wrinkles look, but you don't have to let them take you down either. You can appreciate how beautiful you are right now, thank your wrinkles for being proud proof of a life full of laughter, see them as wisdom watermarks, and notice all the skin on your face that is presently wrinkle-free.

Take a moment right now to close your eyes, breathe deeply, and come up with ten things you're grateful for. Think about the people who love you, the fact that you can read, your health, flowers, the food in your fridge, music, laughter, life lessons, all of it. Really sink into your gratitude and notice whether you feel lighter, whether you feel more centered, relaxed, connected, powerful, loving, and flabbergasted by how blessed you are. Also notice whether you feel a tingle of joy somewhere in your body, and if so, put your hand there and spend a moment connecting with that physical sensation of gratitude. Extra points if you can conjure up some tears. Think of how different your life would be if you walked around in this energy on a regular basis.

This feeling is always available to you—you just have to remain aware enough to make the choice to participate in your gratitude, which is what we're going to practice today. Write down ten reasons why you're grateful that you get to do your habit, not that you *have* to do it, and tap into how this makes you feel physically and emotionally. As the days wear on and the novelty of your habit wears off, remembering to be grateful instead of grumpy can be the difference between sticking with it and throwing in the towel. For example, you can be focused on how hellishly boring it is to be all healthy and eat yet another leaf of spinach, tortured by thoughts of how you'd rather have a loaf of toast, how if you hear the word "organic" one more time you're going to scream, how stuffing your face with a burger and fries just this one day is no big deal in the grand scheme of things, OR you can focus on being grateful that:

- You have this miraculous body that knows how to pump blood through its veins, and can dance, grow hair, heal, feel pleasure, taste a delicious glass of wine, and knit an awesome scarf.

- You're mastering the art of manifesting the reality you choose to live in rather than settling for what you can get.

- You get to nourish your one and only beautiful body.

- You're privy to the magic trick of manifesting what you desire through focus and taking the right action.

- You're changing your life for the better right this very moment.

- You're making your neighborhood a happier place to be by running through it every morning looking so cheerful and fit and healthy.

- You're inspiring everyone around you by showing them that if you can end your love affair with Fritos and take better care of your body, they can make positive changes too.

You have the power and choice to become anybody you choose to become. I mean, think about that—that is one hell of a gigantic birthday present from the Universe, if you ask me. Practice being grateful that you get to make conscious choices, that you've experienced temporary failure so you could learn from it; be grateful for your mind, body, and soul and for the person you're becoming. Use this feeling of gratitude to stay motivated and to defy boredom so you can victoriously lock your habit into place.

Please say your mantra right now. Say it out loud, say it to yourself, say it all day long. Feel it, see it, love it, believe it, rejoice in it, become it, repeat it, and then repeat it some more. Say it right before you fall asleep and first thing when you wake up.

DAY 18: PAY IT FORWARD

I'm writing this book as the COVID-19 pandemic tears through the globe, holed up in my house with who knows what version of life awaiting us all on the other side. I bounce around from feeling sick to my stomach to grateful to focused to human to lying facedown under my desk to creeped out to human to angry to floating in a soap bubble through outer space to determined to devastated to human. Yes, we all feel many of the feels all day long, but everything is heightened right now, and for me, this sense of being human—mortal, mindful, a member of the human family, and one with the collective consciousness—is especially large and center stage, more so than ever. For the first time in my life, every human on Earth is united in the fight against a common enemy (granted, with vastly different resources), and the threat of losing everything from our livelihoods to our lives has stripped existence down to a single profound opportunity to come together, to comfort and protect one another, and to help however we can.

Where we are now reminds me of when I lived in Los Angeles and every so often we'd have an earthquake. The planet would literally shake us awake, yank us out of our heads, and remind us of the preciousness of life, the uncertainty surrounding us in every moment, and all the many things we take for granted that we could be so grateful for. Once the shaking stopped, everyone would leave their homes in a daze (and usually in a bathrobe) and gather in the streets. I'd meet neighbors I'd never met before, hug strangers, talk to everyone like we all went to summer camp together, all of us hovering in this suspended reality—the priorities of connection, general well-being, and gratitude having risen to the surface above the din of our normal concerns, petty obsessions, and social fortresses.

This boiling down of your focus to what's most important and being in an altered state of blisslike appreciation for yourself and your habit is what I'd like to focus on today. It may seem rather highfalutin to attach such profundity to your goal of habitually making your bed every morning, but your commitment to bettering yourself, to consciously shifting your reality, to making manifest the desires in your heart goes way beyond well-fluffed pillows and expertly tucked-in hospital corners.

Stop and think about all the lives you'll impact by becoming a better version of yourself. While you're not in control of how others perceive you or how they act, you are in control of what you model for them and of the opportunities you give them to wake up to their own magnificence. Imagine the message you send out to the world by being a nonsmoker versus being a smoker. Think of how you've shown your friends and family the power of the human mind and of how psyched they are to be free from the stink and the carcinogens. Think of the energy you walk into a room with when you're in shape, eating healthy, appreciative of your miraculous body, versus being schlumpy, in denial, and treating your body like a trash can. Think about what you've taught your children by breaking yourself out of the habit of being broke and becoming someone who rakes in the dough.

Studies have proven that people feel much more satisfaction and happiness when they give gifts than when they receive them, and today I'd like you to use your natural generosity to anchor in your habit and stay on track. All day today, practice feeling into how much you're giving to the world around you by becoming the best version of yourself.

- **Remember that every action you take is like a raindrop in the ocean; no matter how tiny what**

you're doing may seem, it influences the whole. Write down whose lives you're positively affecting by upgrading your life and how you're affecting them. Go way beyond the people immediately surrounding you and take into consideration the ripple effect you'll have on social media, on strangers on the street, on the human race as a whole.

- **All day today, tap into how it feels to give to others, to inspire them, and to offer up the proof that** *if my mocha-latte-lovin' ass can successfully give up caffeine, you can do anything.* Stop, get quiet, and breathe into the gratitude you feel for who you are, for the countless gifts you've been given, and for your ability to offer a motivational kick in the butt to your fellow humans.

- **Go about performing your habit today with the awareness that the Universe is working through you.** Keep in mind that your desires were lovingly given to you so you'd have an exciting purpose to carry out during your stint here on Earth. Remember that by pooh-poohing your excuses and bringing your A game to your habit, you're shining a light that makes it possible for others to see their true selves as well.

Please say your mantra right now. Say it out loud, say it to yourself, say it all day long. Feel it, see it, love it, believe it, rejoice in it, become it, repeat it, and then repeat it some more. Say it right before you fall asleep and first thing when you wake up.

DAY 19: STICK LIKE GLUE

Any change worth making is going to be challenging because it requires you to leap into the unknown. No pain, no gain, as 'twere. It's like when I was busy growing to my full height of six foot one over the course of several short years in high school—I'd wake up screaming in severe charley-horse pain most nights, frantically detangling myself from the sheets to leap out of bed and stretch against the wall. Once I was done growing, the pain stopped and my new height became normal, unremarkable, noticeable to me only when people comment on how tall I am (every day), when I stand at a concert next to a shorter friend who sees only necks and backs, or when I head out on the daunting quest to find and purchase pants long enough to fit me.

At some point, your habit will also become normal, automatic, just another admirable part of who you are. The key is staying the course through the difficult times, which is what we're focusing on today. Tenacity is the number-one thing successful people talk about when asked how they got to where they're at. They credit their success to repeatedly leaping over hurdles; to being the last person standing; to rebuilding when it all falls apart; to turning a deaf ear to the naysayers; to refusing to quit, ever, no matter how gnarly or boring or humiliating things get.

> Success favors the stubborn.

Here are some of the best ways to tap into your most superbly stubborn self:

1. **Anticipate and defuse the discomfort.** Change is challenging for us humans, which is an unfortunate fact considering that the only constant thing in our lives *is* change. If you can't beat change, which you can't, you might as well join it by expecting it, embracing it, and not being so freaked out by it. Your new habit is changing an old way of being, so prepare yourself by meeting your bubbling drama with calm expectation instead of a whole lot of craziness—*Oh look at that, I want a cocktail so bad I'm crawling out of my skin. I'm going to wait until this*

feeling passes instead of alerting everyone to how much I want a drink and how hard this is for me right now. Oh look at that, I'm still ten push-ups away from finishing my workout routine for the day. I want to scream but I reckon I'll just keep going instead because this will all be over in about two minutes. Oh look at that, I'm about to freak out because I've been sitting here writing for ten minutes and each word sucks harder than the next. I'm going to keep writing instead of spiraling off into darkness and self-loathing because eventually something brilliant will hit the page.

> Drama dies without an audience.

Meet your drama with unimpressed expectation and it will lose its power to entangle you.

2. **Practice patience.** I will never forget a sign that I saw in a restaurant when I was visiting India ages ago that read: REMEMBER THE THREE TS: THINGS TAKE TIME. I also remember waiting five hours for a train in Udaipur, taking a two-hour bus ride to Delhi from Agra that lasted eight hours, and hanging out in some government office in Delhi for

two days to get a replacement visa when I lost my passport. Things did indeed take time, but because I was so excited to be there and because everything was new and because sometimes an elephant walked by, I found it fairly easy to fend off my impatience and revel in the moment. *I'm in India! How cool is this?!*

The opportunity to choose patience is always available to us. For example, we can choose, while waiting for over twenty minutes for our spouse to finish up his damn phone call so we can leave for dinner, to be patient and think: *Right now he's talking to someone halfway across the country via cell-phone waves or whatever the hell they're called. Invisible waves that carry our voices all the way around the world! I'm in the presence of a full-blown miracle!*

> Patience is a choice.

Today I want you to practice focusing on the magnificent details, the many miracles in each moment, instead of focusing on how long it's taking to drop the pounds or how bored you are by keeping your house tidy and organized or how tedious it is to go over your finances every week. Notice instead how your brain is working to lock in the list of French vocabulary words you're memorizing and marvel at the fact that you can learn an entirely different language. Notice how healthy your body is becoming and how good your skin feels now that you're eating well. Notice how tight your butt cheeks are getting now that you always take the stairs instead of the elevator. There are infinite things to be grateful for in each moment. Practice focusing on these gifts and on lifting your spirits instead of twisting into a knot of impatience by focusing on what's irritating you.

Please also stay aware of your impatient words today. Stop declaring that you're sick of not partying or whining about how you'd rather take a bullet than another yoga class or how it's taking forever to get your website up. Conversely, please also stay aware of declaring victory too soon and setting yourself up for a crash. Just stay in the moment today by training your thoughts, actions, and words on being grateful for what *is*.

One last tip for becoming a master at patience: breathe. Remember to breathe deeply, relax, and lighten up. Habits take time; choose to enjoy the journey.

3. **Find a tool.** We humans are famous for our love of tools, and today I encourage you to look around and see what some brilliant earthling and fellow habit honer came up

with to make life easier and help y'all stay the course. For example, have you tried using a Fitbit and keeping track of your steps, if you're getting into the habit of walking more? Have you looked into joining Weight Watchers or online business classes or a Zen center or a hiking group to help yourself stay accountable? What about apps? There's literally an app for everything—exercise apps, meditation apps, accountability apps, calorie-counting apps, breathing apps, apps that watch you sleep. . . . See what's out there and download something to help you.

Chances are excellent that you're not the first human to take on whatever habit you're taking on right now.

> Enjoy the camaraderie of knowing that others have gone before you, and that some are attempting the very thing you're attempting right now.

Be grateful that someone who's already headed down the habit highway faced the same issues you're facing and perhaps came up with something to lighten the load. Spend some time researching what tools are out there instead of trying to reinvent the wheel or making things harder on yourself. You are not alone and help is all around you.

4. **Fine-tune the friction.** Revisit the exercises from Day 2 and see if you can come up with some way to make your habit easier if you're adopting a new one or harder if you're breaking a bad one. Really push yourself to come up with one more thing, because ease and friction are some of the most powerful tools when it comes to habits. Can you set up a daily check-in with someone or delete your social media apps or put your coffee maker on your writing desk to help you stay on course? Please come up with one more way to set yourself up for success today and put it into place.

5. **Make struggle your pal.** The Universe gave you the desire to become who you're becoming, the means to create what you desire, and some very creative obstacles to make you strong, to help you learn, and to keep things interesting. Practice being grateful for every temptation, every hiccup, every squirm, by realizing it's there for your benefit. Trust that everything happens for a reason, find the lesson, and appreciate the opportunity to grow instead of feeling angry or frustrated or sorry for yourself.

You don't have to love swimming sixty laps or chewing on yet another raw carrot or ordering a Shirley Temple, but you also don't have to whine about it. Our choices make us who we are, so if you want to be someone with excellent willpower, get good at choosing to focus on the benefits rather than on the buzzkills of the obstacles in your path.

. . . .

Please say your mantra right now. Say it out loud, say it to yourself, say it all day long. Feel it, see it, love it, believe it, rejoice in it, become it, repeat it, and then repeat it some more. Say it right before you fall asleep and first thing when you wake up.

. . . .

DAY 20: SURRENDER

I recently heard a great story from a former client of mine named Carla who, along with trying to get her book published and her chiropractic practice up and running, was struggling with her teenage daughter. Her kid was lethargic, monosyllabic, and interested in nothing but playing with her phone, talking to her friends, and sleeping. Carla tried everything she could think of to get her daughter to engage; she had countless talks with her, sent her to therapists and nature camps, read articles, took away her phone, gave it back, screamed, wept, pleaded, demanded, and grew some premature gray hairs. Carla was consumed by worry and frustration, and for years nothing seemed to change, until one day she finally threw up her hands, sent her daughter off to a strict boarding school, and hoped for the best.

I'm not going to pretend I'm an expert in child psychology (far from it), but I do know that, along with showing up fully and doing everything we know how to do, we also must surrender, release the need to control, and energetically make room for the Universe to give us what we're asking for.

Have you ever had an experience where you're pursuing someone you want to date or you're trying to get pregnant or you're obsessed with getting on a certain podcast or getting a foot in the door to some job and no matter what you try, it just ain't happening? So you finally let it go and stop trying so hard and all of a sudden the person who never gave you the time of day asks you out, the pregnancy test comes back positive, the producer/human resource person calls and asks if you'd come in? When we're working toward manifesting something that's important to us, if we're not careful we can, often unconsciously, become obsessed with thoughts that it's taking too long or that it's not working or that maybe it will never happen for us. Once you surrender, however, you unhook yourself from the negative energy of these thoughts—as if you're being electrocuted and someone shoves you away from the deadly current with a two-by-four—and suddenly you're no longer held captive by desperation, doubt, and disappointment, and a whole new world opens up you.

Carla told me that not only was her daughter getting good grades at the new school, engaging with the other students, and basically coming back to life, but her own professional life was suddenly thriving. She said it was almost creepy—the moment she dropped her daughter off at school, surrendered the need to manage her daughter's life, and set them both free, Carla started getting new clients out of the blue, the money started flowing in almost effortlessly, and her book, which she'd spent the past year diligently trying and failing to get published, was eagerly scooped up by a publisher who was not only a huge fan of her writing but who specialized in precisely the kinds of books she was interested in writing. Carla's also on better terms with her kid; the time apart gave them some much-needed breathing room to reconnect, and Carla's now back to going gray at a normal rate.

> Get out of the way and into the flow.

Today I want you to trade in any doubts, frustration, and impatience you have around your habit for ease, joy, and trust in the universe. What you focus on you create more of, so I want you spend the day focusing on the fact that you don't have to focus on your habit because it's part of who you are. Do the delicate dance of taking action while also remaining detached from the outcome by:

1. **Acting as if.** We've worked on acting as if you're already the person you're becoming, but today I want you to do it as you perform your habit (or refuse to perform an ex-habit). As you go through the motions of your habit, give it as little thought as possible. Treat it like *Oh this old thing?* Ignore it. Confidently assume that of course you behave this way because it's who you are.

2. **Practicing gratitude.** Be grateful that you're already who you strive to be, that this habit is a part of you, that you're effortlessly living the life you set out to live, that everything you desire is hurtling toward you right now. Being in a state of gratitude is one of the most powerful ways to surrender because you can't be in a state of gratitude and be desperate at the same time. Gratitude puts you in the present moment and raises your frequency above any judgments about failures in your past and any anxiety about screwing it up in the future. Gratitude basically allows you to lean back, quiet your mind, and finally receive everything you've been working toward.

3. **Practicing trust/letting go.** Surrender and rigid control are opposite sides of the same energy. Control is resistance. Surrender is acceptance. Control is believing you know what's best. Surrender is believing the Universe is

working through you. Control is fear. Surrender is faith. When we forcefully go after what we want, white-knuckle it, push push push to the point of exhaustion, we risk losing our connection to our desires and connect instead to our fear and lack. What you resist persists—when you resist the temptation to sleep in, resist eating a bowl of macaroni and cheese, resist the urge to binge-watch TV, you are focused on what you don't want/can't have instead of what you're excited about. Surrendering allows you to detach from fear and open up and focus on infinite possibility. Again, this is a delicate dance because we absolutely need to take focused action to achieve our goals, but we must do it from a place of surrender and trust and excited expectation.

Today as you practice your habit, be on the lookout for any fear of failure, fear of past mistakes repeating themselves, or frustration that it's taking too long, and retrain your focus on more powerful thoughts of progress, your incredible ability to change, and the great gift that is your life.

4. **Practicing meditation.** Yep, once again, ye olde sit down and shut up is the road to success. Even five minutes of meditating a day can help you connect to the peace and power that's always available to you (as

opposed to staying hooked by the distractions and the fear). Close your eyes, keep gently moving aside all the thoughts that come into your head, and surrender the reins to the Universe.

Please say your mantra right now. Say it out loud, say it to yourself, say it all day long. Feel it, see it, love it, believe it, rejoice in it, become it, repeat it, and then repeat it some more. Say it right before you fall asleep and first thing when you wake up.

DAY 21: RINSE, REVIEW, REJOICE, REPEAT

T a-da! Today calls for a celebration. Whether you made it all the way through the 21 days with flying colors or dropped a few balls here and there, the important thing is that you're still showing up. Celebrate (I mean it) by coming up with some sort of meaningful something—run a victory lap around your living room or go out for a fancy dinner or announce your success to your social media minions or send yourself a fruit basket. We've become experts at beating ourselves up for our failures and yawning in the face of our achievements—'tis somehow nobler to self-deprecate than to self-celebrate—so do let's make the choice to flip this around right now. Remember, habits are all about who you're being, so be the kind of person who's in the habit of forgiving your failures and appreciating your awesomeness. Write down how you're marking this momentous occasion and then go do it.

Today I'd also like you to read through your notebook and make a cheat sheet of which exercises worked best for you so you have all of your most powerful tools in one place—making a bet with someone terrifying, tracking your habits, leaving your cell phone in the car while you work, or landing a gig on a cruise ship to perform your as-yet-unwritten stand-up routine. Get clear on the specifics of each daily exercise that helped you stick with this new habit and repeat them until your habit becomes a no-brainer. Maybe you've decided you need to do all 21 days again, maybe you've boiled your routine down to a handful of exercises, maybe you've mastered your habit and are ready to fly solo—wherever you're at, the clearer you are, the more successful you will be.

Lastly, please review your mantra, and if you need to upgrade it, do so. You're no longer at the beginning of this process, and the words in your mantra that once struck an emotional chord with you may not be so powerful now that your habit's been on repeat for a few weeks. For example, let's say your mantra is *Money flows to me easily and freely* and, thanks to you and your not-screwing-aroundness, you've anchored in the habit of bringing in more money on a regular basis. You may not yet be where you desire to be financially but you've ditched your cranky old belief that it's hard for you to make money and are now the kind of person who makes it pretty easily. Go back to Day 1 and feel into your desire to make more money and see what comes up for you now that you've peeled back the first layer of *It's hard for me to make money.*

Maybe now that you've got the money coming in, you realize you're scared it won't stick around or will stop coming, so your new mantra is something like *Money flows to me consistently and is always here for me.* Figure out where you're at now—new level, new devil—and if your mantra needs a face-lift, get on it.

We're all in the school of life, and you're spending your one and only shot at being the you who is you going for an A instead of hanging out on the smoking patio and convincing yourself it's cool to settle for a B or a C+. That right there is something to celebrate.

· ·

> Please say your mantra right now. Say it out loud, say it to yourself, say it all day long. Feel it, see it, love it, believe it, rejoice in it, become it, repeat it, and then repeat it some more. Say it right before you fall asleep and first thing when you wake up.

· ·

GOT INTO THE HABIT OF
SETTING GOALS, LISA, 36

I always thought goals were what type A personalities had, and that's so not who I am. I didn't want to be pigeonholed into having a baby in five years or becoming a successful what-the-fuck-ever in two years. But then I found myself in a bad relationship and I couldn't leave because I was working in nonprofit at the time and didn't have the money to move out, so I had to really think about how I could take care of myself and change my situation. So I realized, *Shit, I have to set some goals.*

I didn't even realize it but I was in the habit of just taking things as they came. I was in denial about the fact that I wasn't in control of my life; I didn't want to face my problems and take responsibility, and as a result I wound up in a miserable situation. So I made the decision to set goals and get into the habit of making conscious, smart choices about my life instead of blowing off dealing with things and just hoping it all worked out.

My first goal was to take a real estate course and pass the test—did that. Then I made myself commit to one year of this new career to see if I liked it. I kept focused and was patient and took it one step at a time. It's not easy creating a new path for yourself. . . . It's painful and uncomfortable but so worth it, RIGHT?! The biggest change I made was around my mindset. I am as cynical as they come, but I actually did a fucking vision board. It's true. I clipped tiny pictures of things like the pizza I wanted to eat on my trip to Italy and the house I wanted to live in, pasted them on cardboard—and sure enough that shit came true. I decided that I could be open to new ways of thinking, open to exposing my insecurities and asking for help, I could even be open to yelling I'M READY into the air surrounded by strangers if I had to. Whatever it took, I did it.

> It's usually the stuff you want to do the least that changes your life the most.

I set goals around the amount of money I wanted to make; I made a goal of selling at least one house per month, starting a 401K, buying a house, traveling, and giving more money to charities. I started to meditate and send good energy to myself so I could pull off my goals. I started to articulate my goals and stopped thinking money is evil. I started donating more. My self-worth changed in many ways, and I was able to leave my relationship and have space for myself to grow.

Now I'm even more successful than I set out to be. I actually love my job, doubled my original goal, and now sell at least two houses a month. I just took my qualifying broker's license so I can start my own business and I set new goals all the damn time. Big ones. Don't stop believing. Cue soundtrack.

CHAPTER 5

THE AUDACITY TO BE
YOURSELF

I remember being in my twenties and hanging out in my Manhattan apartment with my boyfriend at the time, looking through a giant bowlful of photographs that I kept on a table in my living room. I'd dumped a couple of hundred pictures from various parts of my life in there, and while we sat and drank beers and sifted through them, I was actually only fake-sifting through them. What I was really doing was sneaking any picture where I looked sexy or cool or world-travel-y to the top of the pile so he'd be sure to see it. To my great frustration, however, he kept digging deep into the bowl, oblivious to my offerings, and ended up pulling out a picture of me at around age sixteen, standing in my friend's driveway with ratty long hair, twiggy arms, not a breast yet in sight, wearing a blue T-shirt that said TO A TENNIS PLAYER, LOVE MEANS NOTHING. In the picture I'm also eating a bag of Doritos, helpless laughter exploding through my big, nacho-cheesy smile.

I tried to casually insert a picture of myself onstage wearing a miniskirt and an electric guitar into his hand. *OMG, I have to tell you the craziest story about this night . . .* but he just moved the one he was already holding even closer to his face to get a better look.

"What is so fascinating about that picture?" I asked, not caring at all.

"I don't know," he said, "there's just something I love about it. I guess it just really looks like you."

This whole self-development thing—upgrading your habits, pushing yourself outside your comfort zone, expanding your perception of reality, being a badass—isn't a competition or some socially dictated finish line you cross that means you've finally "made it." Nor is the quest to better yourself supposed to make you feel like a loser if you're not thinking positive thoughts, or staying laser focused on your clearly defined goals, or clicking your heels with overflowing self-love and happiness 24/7 (can you imagine how annoying *that* person would be to be around?).

All this work is about giving yourself the room, the means, the information, the motivation, and the permission to be the most authentic expression of who you truly are.

Being authentic means loving who you love, pursuing the stuff you're interested in, laughing at the shit you find funny, and fighting for what you think is right. Being authentic also means giving yourself permission to change your mind, to make mistakes, to be a jerk, to beg forgiveness, to be sad, lonely, stupid, and lazy. True authenticity means embracing your whole self, the you who's wearing a miniskirt rocking out onstage *and* the you that's eating a bag of Doritos wondering when the hell puberty is going to show up.

As you do this work, see the habits that you're cultivating as opportunities to let the rare gems of your authenticity shine through, instead of viewing them as proof that you're finally becoming a disciplined, and therefore more socially acceptable, person.

> Forming good habits isn't about being perfect; it's about being more of who you are.

For example, getting into the habit of writing every morning is about expressing your desire to connect with other people through your words, words that are in your voice and that bravely share your wild and weird perspective on the world with your readers. Getting into the habit of eating better and losing weight is about your desire to feel lighter, healthier, and more connected to the physical manifestation of your one and only self, otherwise known as your body. Even getting into the habit of doing the damn dishes every night is about your desire to restore order to your life, to treat yourself and your surroundings like they matter, to make the world a better, more ant-free place.

As you go through the habit-forming process, you will hit oil slicks on your road to success—you'll stay snuggly in bed and blow off running on the treadmill before work and you will erupt into a tirade of expletives behind the wheel of your car, contrary to your no-being-an-a-hole decree. The question is not whether you'll slip up but how you'll choose to respond when you do. Getting back on track with your habit ASAP is critical, but how about if you also spend the time you usually reserve for beating yourself up or whining about what a dope you are on immediately forgiving yourself instead? What if you included, with all future habits that you embark on, the bonus habit of allowing yourself to be human and therefore flawed?

> What if you had the kind of compassion for yourself that you tend to reserve for other people?

I've peppered this book with stories about real people who recognized a habit they wanted to change and got their mindset into a place where they could attack that goal like their pants were on fire. And while I love hearing all the inspirational details of how we humans pull off success, keep in mind that it's easier to see the progression of a process like habit forming/breaking when you've got the advantage of hindsight and the ability to leave out the details of the massive slipups and buffoonery that we all experience along the way. Not only were these people able to look back and see how their habit anchored in but they could notice how even some coincidences and activities that seemed totally unrelated at the time served to reinforce the new behavior pattern they were pursuing.

When you're bravely forging through this process, you might not be able to recognize the tricks that help you sidle past obstacles, or how your new obsession with waking up and charting the progress of the anthill behind your garage is helping you get centered before sitting down to study every morning. Trust your intuition, don't question stuff that feels good if it's not harming your progress, and remember that just showing up and giving it your best shot is an act worthy of a round of applause.

We live in a culture obsessed with achievement and goals. And while I loves me some good, solid gettin' 'er done, I do not love it at the expense of our own self-worth. We need to deny the overpopular trend of smearing fear and shame all over ourselves and instead celebrate compassion, colossal screwups, and vulnerability. Think about the people in your life who you love. You're inspired by them when they do great things, you're blown away when they face their fears, and you dance around them in circles when they ace the bar exam. But you also love your peeps for the fact that they don't realize they have some salsa stuck to their lip and that they cry at graduations and that they look so scared and lost when faced with downloading a new operating system onto their computer.

Real human connection happens when we're vulnerable, not when we're being handed a gold medal. I believe that this natural pull toward vulnerability is why we literally can't stop staring at babies. Babies are cute and all (usually; I've certainly seen some that look like turtles or fat truck drivers), but I think we're mesmerized by how fragile, exposed, and helpless they are. Staring at a baby is like plugging into the motherlode of human vulnerability; it's a force so compelling we literally can't take our eyes off it until the baby's mom yanks at the stroller, hurries off, and shoots us a look like she's memorizing our face, just in case.

We all have a little fleshy baby inside of us that we've covered up over the years in order to survive. And while a world full of adults stumbling around all openly vulnerable and helpless would not serve anyone well, we've swung too far the other way. We've made a habit out of being scared and ashamed of these softer parts of ourselves, which cuts us off from the connection, serenity, and happiness we so deeply desire.

Use this journey of forming habits that you love as a way to go beyond just the noble achievement of a goal and to forge a more intimate relationship with your most authentic self. Understand that embracing who you truly are is about accepting yourself through all of it—when you're at your most victorious, your most irritable, your most temper-tantrumy, and your most vulnerable.

> Self-love isn't about being perfect.

Give yourself the permission to be, to do, and to have whatever lights up your heart and practice forgiving your screwups along the way. Loving your whole self is simply a habit, a habit that's definitely worth having.

ACKNOWLEDGMENTS

Thanks to all you badasses who keep showing up to do the work. When you change your life, you change countless lives around you, and you sure as hell have changed mine so thank you thank you thank you! Thanks to everyone who contributed their personal stories and helped me write this book—those whose stories I included and those I didn't. For anonymity's sake I won't name names, but I couldn't have done this without you and I so appreciate you taking the time to do me this massive favor. Thanks to my amazing editor, Laura Tisdel, who has birthed books with me through thick and never thin. I do believe this time around was the thickest (and yet still so fun)! Thanks to my brilliant agent, Alexandra Machinist, for always having my back and for making doing business feel like having cocktails with my bestie. Thanks to Team Amazeballs: Nate Meltzer, Shannon Twomey,

ACKNOWLEDGMENTS

Lydia Hirt, Ciara Johnson, Shelby Meizlik, Brooke Halsted, Gabriel Levinson, Jason Ramirez, Jane Cavolina, Cassandra Garruzzo, Hilary Roberts, and Meredith Clark. Thanks to Rembert and Squiggle Block, the best pandemic pals ever, for keeping me company and somewhat sane while writing this book. Thanks to my incredible biological and chosen family for your love and support over the years. There are too many of you to mention but I'd like to thank a few in particular who have helped me become a better writer and speaker and whom I borrow (steal?) zingers from on the reg: Mom, Dad, Steve, Jill, Bob, Cynthia Greenberg, Tania Katan, Elissa Breitbard, Kim Green, and Tami Abts. Thanks to Gecko for, among so many other things, keeping me grounded during all the writing/touring/home renovation storms. Thanks to Shannon Waldner, my first witch.

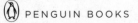